# Christmas
## at Historic Houses

Schiffer Publishing Ltd®

4880 Lower Valley Road, Atglen, Pennsylvania 19310

Patricia Hart McMillan
Katharine Kaye McMillan

Designed by Stephanie Daugherty
Type set in Champignon/Garamond/Neutra Display/Italian Cursive, 16th c./Christmas

ISBN: 978-0-7643-3559-4
Printed in China

Schiffer Books are available at special discounts for bulk purchases for sales promotions or premiums. Special editions, including personalized covers, corporate imprints, and excerpts can be created in large quantities for special needs. For more information contact the publisher:

Schiffer Publishing Ltd.
4880 Lower Valley Road
Atglen, PA 19310
Phone: (610) 593-1777; Fax: (610) 593-2002
E-mail: Info@schifferbooks.com

For the largest selection of fine reference books on this and related subjects, please visit our web site at

**www.schifferbooks.com**

We are always looking for people to write books on new and related subjects. If you have an idea for a book please contact us at the above address.

This book may be purchased from the publisher. Include $5.00 for shipping. Please try your bookstore first. You may write for a free catalog.

In Europe, Schiffer books are distributed by

Bushwood Books
6 Marksbury Ave.
Kew Gardens
Surrey TW9 4JF England
Phone: 44 (0) 20 8392 8585; Fax: 44 (0) 20 8392 9876
E-mail: info@bushwoodbooks.co.uk
Website: www.bushwoodbooks.co.uk

# Dedications

To Louise Decker

*"a* **worthy** *woman...
her price is far above rubies..."*

– Proverbs 31:10 KJV

Fear not, for behold,
I bring you good tidings of great joy,
which shall be to all people,
For unto you is born this day
in the city of David,

a **Savior**,

which is Christ the Lord.

– Luke 2:10, King James Version

# Acknowledgments

Our deep gratitude to Tina Skinner for her faith in this book, and to Editor Nancy Schiffer for seeing it to fruition. Special thanks to Roger Torres, guru, and the wonderful people who keep historic houses living history.

*Adams House* Mary A. Kopco, Kate Bentham, Rose Speirs

*Bidwell* Martha L. Dailey

*Baldwin-Reynolds* Joshua F. Sherretts

*Bartow-Pell Mansion* Amanda Kraemer

*Billings Farm* Susan Plump

*Biltmore* Kathleen Mosher, Andy Pearce, Erica Daves,

*Bingham-Waggoner Estate* Janeen Aggen

*Blithewold* Eileen Miller

*Butterworth Center & Deere-Wiman House* Angela Hunt

*Calvin B. Taylor,* Edward H. Hammond, Jr., Susan Taylor

*Campbell Hou*se ( St. Louis) Andy Hahn

*Campbell House* ( Spokane) Joyce M. Cameron, Patti Larkin, Marsha Rooney, Jill Strom

*Chief Vann House,* Julia Autra

*Chinqua Penn Plantation,* Lisa Yamaoka Phelps, Yanida Campa at Renegade Holdings, Laura Pearce, Lynn Umstead Crocker, Kim Parr, Marcia Swiderski

*Colonial Williamsburg,* Jim Bradley, Kathy Dunn, Marianne Martin, Kathy Rose, Meredith Sprinkle, Kathy Wallace, Karam Hwang

*David Davis Mansion,* Marcia D. Young, PhD

*Drayton Hall,* Natalie Titcomb

*Flagler Museum,* John Blades, Amanda Wilson

*Florence Griswold House,* Tammi Flynn, Rebecca Giantonio at Pita Communications

*Gallier (Hermann-Grima and Gallier),* Stephen A. Moses, Lisa B. Samuels

*Hazelwood,* Wendy Barszcz, Chris Dunbar

*Hearth Northington Plantation,* George H. Northington IV, Janet Hobizel

*Hearthside Homestead,* Kathryn A. Hartley, *Ruth A.B. Clegg*

*Hearthstone,* Christine A. Cross

*Joel Lane, Raleigh, NC,* Kathleen C. Ruse

*John Lind House,* Trudy Beranek, The Red Hat Ladies

*LBJ Ranch* The Late First Lady, Lady Bird Johnson; Lynda Bird Johnson Robb; Shirley James; Barbara Biffle; Judy Callen; Elizabeth Hansen; Margaret Harman, Sherry Justus, and our dear friend, Simone Poulaine of the U.S. State Department, an adviser to Mrs. Johnson

*Leu,* Robert Bowden, Mantana Brown

*Marjorie Kinnan Rawlings House,*Kathleen E. Carr

*Marshal's Home & Jail,* Janeen Aggen

*Maymont,* Carla Murray, Dale Wheary

*Molly Brown House,* Annie Robb

*Monticello,* Kim Curtis, Sharon McElroy, Wayne Mogielnicki

*Morris-Butler House,* Shannon Borbely

*Mount Clare Museum House,* Michael Connolly, Jane D. Woltereck, and Kathleen G. Kotarba, Baltimore City Department of Planning

*Mount Vernon,* Dawn Bonner, Patty Balladares, Mary V. Thompson

*My Old Kentucky Home,* Alice Heaton, Jean Unglaub

*Oldfields-Lilly House,* Katherine B. Zarich

*Petersen,* Amy A. Douglass

*Pettingill-Morron,* Amy Kelly

*Physick Estate,* Jean Barraclough

*Pittock Mansion,* Lucy Smith McLean

*Richards-DAR,* Sallie M. Grow

*Riversdale,* Ann Wass, PhD

*Samuel Cupples,* Petruta Lipank, Mary Marshall, Bridget Fletcher, Neil Metzger

*Sherwood Davidson,* Emily Larson

*Slifer ,*Gary W. Parks

*Tudor Place,* Heather A. Bartlow

*Vaile Mansion,* Janeen Aggen,

*Van Cortlandt Manor,* Rob Schweitzer

*Waddesdon,* Vicky Darby,

*Wade,* David M. Simmons

*Webb-Deane-Stevens,* Charles T. Lyle

# Contents

# Preface

Like Santa's bag, this book is full of good things for lovers of history, architecture, interior design, art and artifacts, and Christmas! Travel enthusiasts will discover exciting destinations—most with year-round events, all with exciting Christmas and Holiday Season social calendars.

History lovers will learn a great deal about important people and the places, things and key events associated with their homes, which are now museums. In many Houses, there are original documents, including personal letters, journals, ledgers and diaries to examine. Curators, directors, and docents in lectures, presentations, and personal exchanges are sources of endlessly fascinating information.

Architects have long since discovered many of these houses as sources of inspiration and instruction. Monticello, for example, is mecca to those enamored with Jefferson's classicism. The buildings at Colonial Williamsburg, ranging from modest cottages to the Governor's Palace, are a tremendous, continuing influence on American taste in domestic architecture. All the houses in this book have design lessons to teach.

Interior designers may look to Colonial Williamsburg, Biltmore, Waddesdon, and other houses for education and inspiration. These houses might be considered the prototypical "designers' showcases," in that visitors can study all the elements of interior design. Especially interesting are antique color schemes—sometimes surprisingly contemporary! Effective furniture placement—often with a minimal number of pieces—is a lesson beautifully taught and easily learned by all homemakers. At Christmas time, these houses are chock full of easy-to-copy holiday décor ideas. Conveniently, similar decorative items—often reproductions, like the Martha (Washington) chair by Taylor King—may be found in the museums' gift shops or retail stores. This makes it easy to bring home reminders of Christmas past and present.

The historic houses we visit in this book are museums (with one exception: the John Lind House), so expect to see outstanding fine art and unique artifacts. Sometimes there are only a few pieces, but be prepared for breathtaking expansive collections at Colonial Williamsburg, Biltmore, Waddesdon, and others.

This book is especially for those who are devoted to this special holiday season with its deeply spiritual significance. While religious ceremonies of the season first occurred in church, spirituality carried over to the home. We see Santa Claus (formerly St. Nicholas) taking on in secular guise the role of Christ in the giving of gifts as an expression of love, Christ's essential teaching. Gifts also symbolize Christ's greatest gift—His life in return for eternal life promised to all who follow Him. This idea, and Christ's welcome to all, makes Christmas completely joyous, the happiest of holidays. Little wonder that Christmas is the best of times in which to visit Historic Houses.

Keeping
the Past
Enriching

the Future

Historic house museums keep alive the winter social season tradition that began during Colonial times. Most have Christmas as the focal point of **sensational** decorations and gala activities. These give historic house museums designer-showcase glamour, making them *the places to visit* during what many consider to be the most wonderful time of the year. Originally Christmas was Christ Mass, the Christian holy-day observance on December 25th to celebrate the birth of Christ. Later it also became an important secular holiday with the focus on the **family**. We see both religious and secular influences in the decorations of historic houses.

Over 4,500 historical societies and a multitude of individuals in North America, Great Britain and around the world care for historic houses. **Why?** Because the houses are tangible evidence of lives well lived in the pursuit of life, liberty and happiness. More importantly, these relics of the past keep alive the values, ideals, and philosophies that inspired the creative men and women who built houses, families, communities, and nations.

House museums remain vital today as important reminders of events that happen there. Education programs that interpret historic facts, offer insights and inform the future. Education—a year 'round activity—is a key part of Christmas events which feature costumed guides and lecturers who regale visitors with fascinating history, making past events immediate and relevant to this time and place. Educational programs make it very clear that historic house museums are *living* legends.

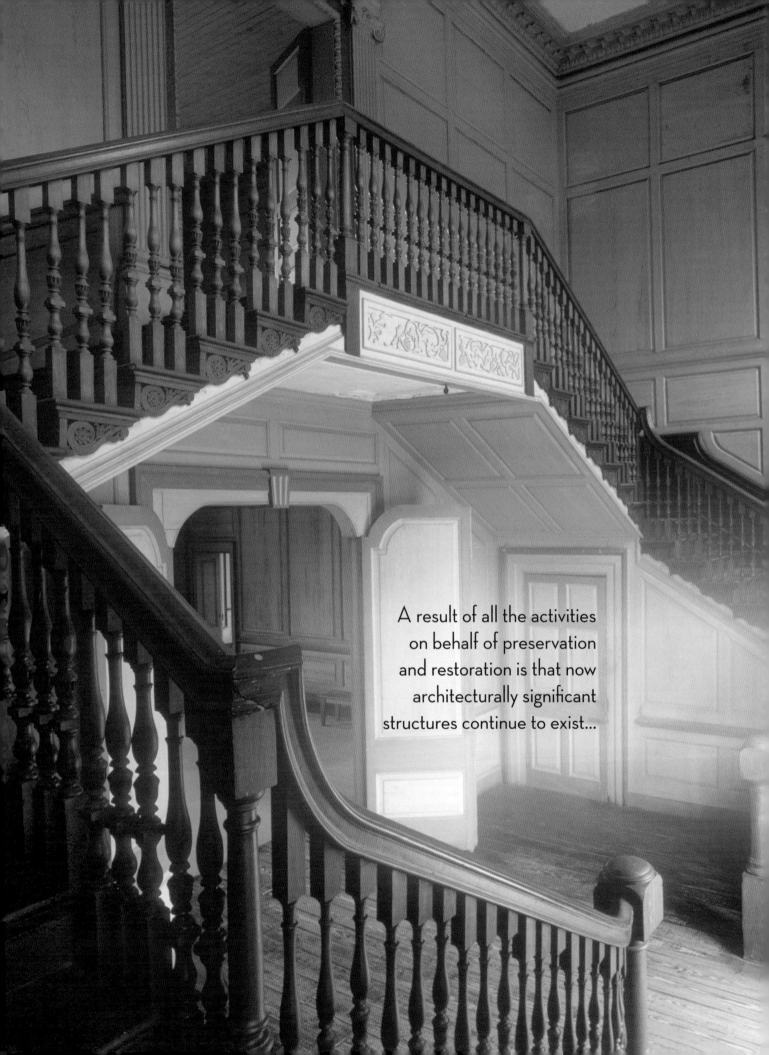

A result of all the activities on behalf of preservation and restoration is that now architecturally significant structures continue to exist...

# Early Restorations

In the United States, efforts to save historically important structures began as early as 1813, when the Philadelphia State House was saved from demolition. But for a nation pushing toward new frontiers, preservation was not a wide-spread notion.

In Virginia, the home of many of the nation's founding fathers, a group of women banded together in 1853 as the Mount Vernon Ladies' Association to save Mount Vernon, the home of George Washington. That Mount Vernon should be left to rot and ruin was unthinkable!

While this group was trying to save Mount Vernon, Monticello, the home of Thomas Jefferson, had been sold out of the Jefferson family and was in poor shape. An unlikely individual came to the rescue. Uriah P. Levy, a career Naval officer and admirer of Jefferson, bought Monticello. Later, it was seized from him by the Confederate government and sold

**Opposite and previous page:** Unmodernized, unfurnished Drayton Hall offers visitors glimpses of "layers of time" in architectural influences of several periods visible in the entry hall and withdrawing room. *Photographs courtesy Drayton Hall, Charleston, South Carolina*

**Above:** Architect Thomas Annan interpreted the heroic H. H. Richardson Romanesque Revival style as domestic architecture in The Samuel Cupples House in Saint Louis—a powerful example of the influence of historic houses. *Photograph courtesy The Samuel Cupples House at Saint Louis University.*

1. Drayton Hall, considered America's finest Georgian-Palladi an structure, is a fitting backdrop for holiday singers of spirituals likely sung centuries ago in surrounding fields. *Photograph courtesy Drayton Hall, Charleston, South Carolina*
2. Hazelwood, the 1837 home of Morgan Lewis Martin in Green Bay, Wisconsin was inspired by his childhood home in New York State, but shares the simple, classic lines of the Nelson Galt Office in Colonial Williamsburg. *Photograph courtesy the Brown County Historical Society.*
3. The simplicity of the Nelson-Galt Office at Colonial Williamsburg has inspired generations of residential structures across the United States. *Photograph courtesy The Colonial Williamsburg Foundation.*
4. Thomas Jefferson's Monticello with its distinctive dome continues to vigorously inform domestic architecture and interior design. *Photograph courtesy Robert C. Laufman/Thomas Jefferson Foundation, Inc.*

again. Levy's estate recovered the property, and when lawsuits were settled in 1879, Uriah's nephew, Jefferson Monroe Levy, a New York Lawyer and member of Congress, took control. He began work to restore and preserve the rapidly deteriorating home. In 1923, The Thomas Jefferson Foundation purchased the home from Jefferson Levy and restored it with the help of leading architects.

It is perhaps impossible to measure the influences that Mount Vernon and Monticello have had on American domestic architecture. It can be seen in such dignified structures as Hazelwood, the Greenbay, Wisconsin home of Martin L. Martin, the president of the Constitution Convention (1847-1848), which resulted in Wisconsin Statehood,

It was not until 1926 that John D. Rockefeller, Jr., at the urging of the Reverend W.A.R. Goodwin, rector of Burton Parish Church, began the enormous project of restoring and preserving Williamsburg, Virginia "as an authentic Colonial village." See a portion of the results of this gargantuan effort in Chapter 13. To see the entire project, visit Colonial Williamsburg, often!

In 1929, Henry Ford established Greenfield Village at Dearborn, Michigan. Not an authentic village, it is a collection of 83 authentic historic buildings assembled on 80 acres; structures include Noah Webster's home (where he wrote the first American dictionary), Thomas Edison's Menlo Park, New Jersey laboratory, and the courthouse where Abraham Lincoln practiced law.

South Carolina designated the nation's first *historic district* in Charleston in 1931; the work of preserving Historic Charleston continues. The National Trust for Historic Preservation was begun in 1949 to preserve sites all across the nation.

None are more interesting than Drayton Hall (now a museum), in Charleston, South Carolina. Construction on this house began in 1738 and it was complete in 1742. Dr. George McDaniel, a recent director of Drayton Hall, has said, "Drayton Hall has witnessed so much history that it is our duty to preserve that history, as best we can, and share it with the public." The house, never modernized, has no running water, electricity, or central heating. It extends a sense of timelessness and continuity, representing "layers of time"—the colonial, Revolutionary War and Civil War periods and the Victorian age. Drayton Hall should be on every historic house lover's *must see* list.

The effort to preserve important sites was made clear in 1966, when Congress passed the National Historic Preservation Act and established a National Register of Historic Places. In 1978, the Revenue Act made possible investment tax credits for rehabilitating historic buildings—a real incentive for not tearing them down.

A result of all the activities on behalf of preservation and restoration is that now architecturally significant structures continue to exist, such as the unique Romanesque-style Samuel Cupples mansion in St. Louis, Missouri, and houses of cultural importance shown throughout this book.

Martha chair by Taylor King

Furnishings in the Nelson Gait office seem fresh and up-to-date. *Photograph courtesy The Colonial Williamsburg Foundation.*

# The White House Finally Passes Muster

$\mathscr{P}$erhaps the preservation effort that most riveted the nation occurred when Mrs. Jacqueline Kennedy moved with her husband, President John F. Kennedy, into the un-stately White House. Truth be told, the interiors of "the people's house" were probably sadder than some of today's cheap motels. Famed decorator Mrs. Henry (Sister) Parish II worked with Mrs. Kennedy to refurbish the private living quarters. But the public areas—far less attractive than Monticello and Mount Vernon, Mrs. Kennedy noted—were in greatest need. And, Mrs. Kennedy was dismayed to discover that there wasn't even a visitor's guide book!

Mrs. Kennedy thought that the White House—the **symbol of the nation**—deserved to be furnished with appropriate antiques. She turned to Winterthur, the Henry du Pont estate in Wilmington, Delaware, which had become a museum, directed by Charles Montgomery (1954-1961). Mr. Murray suggested forming a Fine Arts Committee to acquire worthy antique furnishings for the White House. Henry du Pont, acknowledged as the country's leading authority, chaired that committee.

Mrs. Kennedy began restoration work on the White House by stating her well-considered view; that is, *that everything*

Young Caroline Kennedy stands beside a gloriously decorated 1961 Christmas Tree in the Blue Room at The White House, which was refurbished through the efforts of her mother, First Lady Jacqueline Kennedy. *Photograph by Cecil Stoughton, courtesy the John F. Kennedy Presidential Library and Museum, Boston*

*ought to have a reason for being there—a matter of scholarship, not mere decoration.* In September 1961, Congress passed Public Law 87-286, officially declaring the White House a museum. Many citizens donated valuable antiques and family heirlooms. A Curator's office was established to care for them and to prevent radical (and we might add, careless and uninformed) future change in the interiors. That same year, 1961, The White House Historical Association was formed to oversee White House programs—and to publish a guide book!

Mrs. Kennedy's televised tour of the restored White House was one of the most-watched programs in TV history. Perhaps the restored White House was still no match for Winterthur, Biltmore, or Waddesdon, the Rothschild's country house in England. But for the first time, the White House looked as it should for its role in world affairs. And, of course, it is utterly magical in the Christmas season.

The restoration of most state rooms on the ground and first floors were completed by November 1963, when President Kennedy died. Citizens will always owe a great debt of gratitude to Jacqueline Kennedy for her restoration of "the people's house."

# Christmases in the Restored White House

$\mathscr{M}$rs. Lyndon Baines Johnson—Lady Bird to all—described the restored White House at Christmas eloquently in her diary.

The fragrance of evergreens filled the halls and holly was everywhere, throughout the house—all around the great light fixtures—and there were huge bowls of it on the tables. ... Everybody enjoyed the decorations—the great Christmas tree in the Blue Room and the lovely crèche with seventeenth-century Neapolitan figures in the East room. ... .we went upstairs to the Yellow Oval Room, where the red velvet stockings—now eight—hung from the mantel. ...Our own Christmas tree was covered with icicles and snowflakes and gingerbread men, toy drummers, strings of popcorn (real) and cranberries (not real) and topped with the star that had been on FDR's tree back in the early 1940s. It was beautiful!

In August of 2006, she shared her memories.

The Christmas season is a magical time in the White House! Christmas for the Johnsons always has meant the LBJ Ranch, but during our time when Lyndon was President, we spent two wonderful Christmases at the White House.

During the first, in 1967, we gathered in our favorite Yellow Oval Room on the second floor to open presents around the tree. All eyes were on our darling grandson Lyn (Nugent) and on our two sons-in-law who soon were to leave for service in the Marines and Air Force. Like some lovely fragile bubble, it was a moment to catch and hold and remember.

Firelight danced on the Christmas tree star—the same star that had been used by the Roosevelts when they lived in the White House. Stockings hung from the mantel with symbolic decorations that told an amusing story of each of our lives. Everyone waited with bated breath for their own

# The Historic House List Grows

*T*he list of Historic Houses continues to grow, as their value to society becomes ever more apparent. Traditionally, homes of US presidents are preserved. Most recently, the LBJ Ranch—known as the Texas White House—was added to the list of Historic Houses in America.

Before the death of President Johnson in 1973, he and Mrs. Johnson worked out a plan to donate the LBJ Ranch to the United States, with the proviso that Mrs. Johnson continue to live in the house, and she did so until her death in 2007. In August 2008, the Texas White House at the LBJ Ranch (maintained by the National Park Service) was opened to the public; that is, the public could visit LBJ's office, the dining room and certain other areas while the rest of the house was being restored.

In a second volume of Christmas at Historic Houses, we hope to publish Lynda Bird Johnson Robb's warm and loving recollections of her family's holiday gatherings at The LBJ Ranch. We encourage readers to visit the LBJ Ranch in the scenic Texas Hill Country at Christmas when there's a calendar full of activities—and in the springtime, when one can see the wildflowers that inspired Lady Bird's Beautification program, an enduring legacy.

Lady Bird Johnson with Texas wildflowers on the LBJ Ranch

gifts to be opened. I was anxious to see if Lynda was as pleased with her original edition of Dickens as I hoped she would be, and whether Luci liked the "little boy" suits selected for Lyn as much as we did. And from the ranch, we distributed gifts of jellies and preserves and corn relishes and pickled pears—a beautiful bounty transported north! Lyndon's gifts were the most generous and most glamorous that year and every year. He always was one of Santa's best helpers!

Christmas of 1968 was a particular time of joy for us.

There was a special feeling of closeness to family and friends, and reflections on jobs done with heart and hope along with expectations about the time to come.

We were looking forward to going home to the ranch with its fields of wildflowers to renew us, and for Lyndon to start afresh. He eagerly looked forward to having time for family and self and to, perhaps, teaching again and helping young people prepare for their futures.

That Christmas, our last in the White House and in Washington, was a glorious chapter in our lives that was drawing to a close. So many changes had been wrought in our lives while we lived in that House. Truly, we counted our blessings.

**Each year at Christmas, a grateful nation also counts its blessings—giving thanks for the men who occupy the White House as they assume the burden of the presidency of a democratic nation in which all are free to celebrate Christmas.**

In 1965, President and Mrs. Johnson posed beside their White House Christmas Tree.
*Photograph by Robert Knudsen, courtesy the LBJ Library.*

Annually, some 300,000 visitors pass through these heavily carved doors to view the same treasures that enthralled the Queen of England.

# Restoration and Preservation in England

$\mathcal{T}$he National Trust for Places of Historic Interest or Natural Beauty was formed in England in 1895. It is registered with the express purpose of preserving, for the benefit of the nation, lands and buildings (and furnishings) of beauty or historic interest. In the mid-20th century, interest focused on saving impressive country houses and gardens, endangered because private owners were increasingly unable to maintain these expensive properties.

In the late 1960s, the Trust was accused of placing too much emphasis on these strongholds of aristocracy. But, preserving them as sources of tremendous national pride and inspiration for future generations remains important work. It is successfully argued that these properties—and the aristocracy which created them—represent a crucial part of the nation's—and western culture's—heritage.

Outstanding among many properties under the care of the Trust is Waddesdon, the country home of Baron Ferdinand de Rothschild. Never just an excuse for the display of wealth and power, Waddesdon was a home—one that opened its doors as quickly to London's displaced children during World War II as to the nation's rich and powerful. In 1997, Waddesdon Manor (see Chapter 10) was designated "Best National Trust Property." Waddesdon has also been designated "Museum of the Year, 1997," received the "England for Excellence Silver Award, 1998," the "Euopa Nostra Ward, 1999," "Best Overall Property Silver Award, 1999," "Best Gift Show, 1999," "Excellence in England Silver Award 2002," and "Museums and Heritage Award for Excellence, 2003."

# Funding Preservation and Restoration

$\mathcal{K}$eeping historic houses alive is expensive. Finding necessary funds, even in the best of times, is a challenge. At all Historic Houses, curators and directors provide new and wonderful events throughout the year, every year! Most houses publicize events well ahead of the dates, making it easy to mark one's personal social calendar.

The winter social season—with its heightened air of expectation—is an ideal time for fund-raising efforts that educate and entertain. Imaginative events, like the December 2006 African-American spiritual music concert by Ann Caldwell (a student of June Bonner of the Metropolitan Opera) and The Magnolia Singers at Drayton Hall, draw the public to historic houses.

The concert provided a rare opportunity for music and history lovers to gather in the candlelit great hall. They heard music that could have been heard centuries earlier in the fields and praise houses surrounding Drayton Hall. A catered reception fed guests, who were treated to tours of the house by experienced museum guides—all for a modest price.

**Opposite:** Queen Victoria walked through these doors in 1890, when she accepted Baron de Rothschild's invitation to lunch at Waddesdon Manor. *Photograph by Mike Fear, courtesy Waddesdon Manor*

**Above:** Drayton Hall, a Georgian-Palladi an structure in its original state, provides a treasure of information for arcitects and designers. *Photograph courtesy Drayton Hall, Charleston, South Carolina*

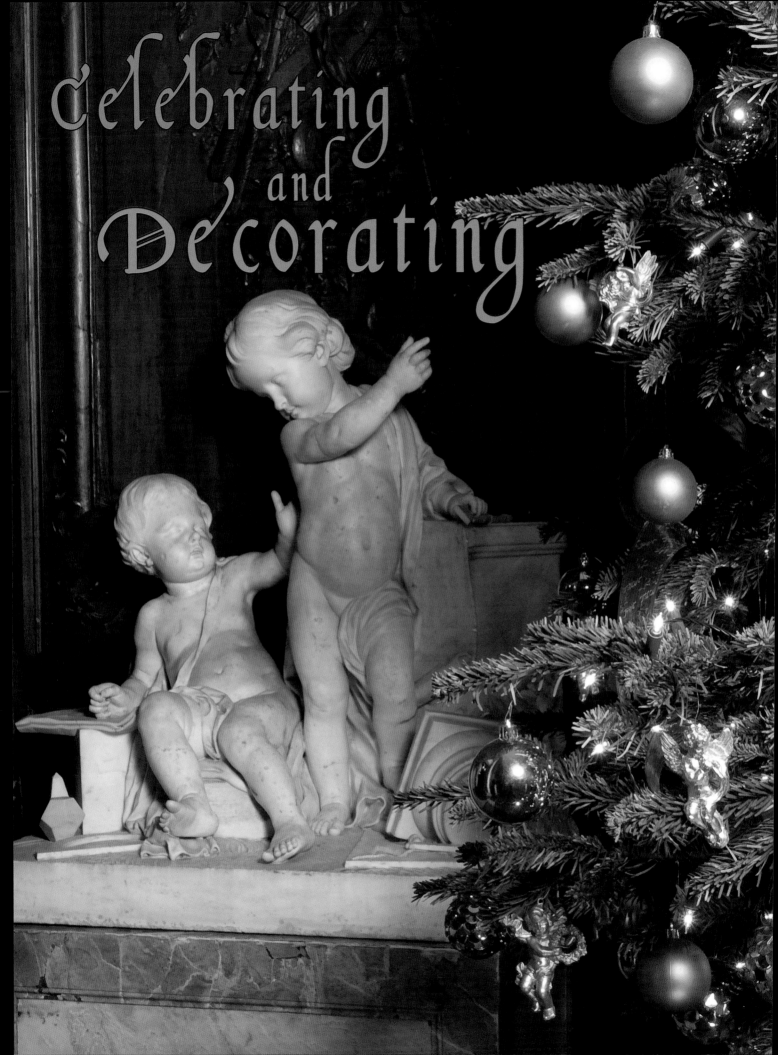

Celebrating
and
Decorating

*H*istoric houses at Christmas time reveal that customs varied from time to time, place to place, and according to religious conviction, financial circumstances, social conditions, and aesthetic tastes. It's interesting to compare the restrained (even Puritanical) decoration of Mount Vernon and Monticello with seasonal evergreen boughs to the extravagant Victorian-style interiors of houses of later eras. During the Victorian age, customs from various countries joined forces to make Christmas the most decorative, most lavishly celebrated of all holidays.

Certainly, the story of the celebration of the birth of Jesus is one of change. The Scriptures describe the birth of Jesus, but do not command its celebration. Nonetheless, until the 4th Century A.D., His birth was celebrated anytime between January and September. Then, Pope Julius 1 chose December 25 as the birthdate of Jesus—a move that appropriated pagan midwinter merrymaking and celebrations for religious purposes. *Christmas* was born.

The Classic
Design

# Customs Through the Years

Customs for celebrating Christmas varied from country to country. In Tudor England, the Christmas period began with St. Nicholas Day (December 6) and ended with Holy Innocents Day (December 28). A Yule Log, lit on Christmas Eve, burned throughout the 12 days of Christmas—a period when common laborers would have time off, perhaps the only respite they would know during the year. Carols telling of the nativity were sung. Feasting—eating and drinking—was important and at times became entirely riotous, to the disgust of the more puritanical Believers.

To many puritanical Christians, the weekly "Lord's Day" (Sunday) commemoration of the death, burial, resurrection and anointing of Jesus as The Christ, Divine Savior and author of eternal life was important, Christmas was not. Some considered it pagan, and the Puritans in the mid-17th century England banned Christmas (and all other celebrations). The restoration of Charles II to the throne of England in 1660 ended the ban.

In the American Colonies, Puritans banned Christmas in Boston from 1659 to 1681. Many who identified Christmas with the English, tended to ignore it. George Washington seemed to have treated Christmas Day as any other day, choosing to attack England's Hessian mercenaries on Christmas at the Battle of Trenton, 1777. Instead of making much of Christmas, the Washingtons celebrated the winter season with festive meals in the striking dining room (see chapter 11) at Mount Vernon, a much visited place as depicted in the painting "Autumn," available in the Mount Vernon gift shop.

Autumn, a painting available at the gift shop at Mount Vernon (opposite), home of George Washington, first President of the United States of America. *Photographs courtesy Mount Vernon Ladies Association*

In Colonial Williamsburg, the Geddy girls read the Bible, a custom continued later by slaves at the Heard-Northington's Egypt Plantation in Texas.

Following the American Revolution, many Americans, including Mary Boardman Crowninshield, whose husband Benjamin was Secretary of the Navy, continued to think that Christmas belonged to the Catholic Church, calling it "their great day."

But public opinion changed, beginning with Clement Moore's *A Visit From St. Nicholas* (*Twas the Night Before Christmas*) poem in 1822, which painted a charming, idyllic picture of Christmas as an event for children. The poem focused on the gift-giving St. Nicholas with no reference to the Christ child. In 1843, *A Christmas Carol* by Charles Dickens romantically pictured Christmas as a time of ideal familial warmth and goodwill to all. But perhaps the most important influencer was the Christmas 1848 picture of Queen Victoria, Prince Albert and their children gathered around a decorated Christmas tree.

According to Dr. Marcia Young, Director of the David Davis House in Bloomington, Illinois, "Our story began during the middle of the nineteenth century. Then, a newer version of Christmas began to be celebrated in the church, because members of the congregation began decorating their houses of worship with evergreens and Christmas trees for the benefit of the children attending the 'Sabbath Schools.' In Springfield, Illinois, where the Abraham Lincolns (lifelong friends of the Davis family) lived in 1859, at least two of the city's churches were decorated with Christmas trees and evergreens—the First Presbyterian Church, where the Lincolns rented a pew, and the Third Presbyterian Church." In 1870, in the United States, Congress declared Christmas a Federal holiday and President Ulysses S. Grant signed it into law.

By the time Christmas became a Federal holiday in the United States, customs from many countries had been widely adopted. Gift-giving was becoming ever more important—to the point where some decried the commercialism of Christmas. Decorations gave vent to creativity, beginning with adopting a palette of red and green colors, hanging wreaths on doors and at windows, placing lighted candles in the windows, hanging stockings by the mantel, creating fanciful arrangements of fruits, and decorating evergreen and other trees, first for the parlor and eventually for every room in the house! Today, we've grown to expect all-out, over-the-top decorations so that houses decorated simply and with restraint are a bit of a shock.

All historic houses at Christmas time, whether simply or lavishly decorated, are powerful reminders of specific times, places and people. Each is a wonderful place to visit during this holiday.

**Above:** Reenacters portray the Geddy daughters at a customary holiday Bible reading session. *Photograph courtesy The Colonial Williamsburg Foundation*
**Left:** For her documentary commemorating Black History Month, television producer Geneva Flora reenacted a slave reading the Bible—a fitting Christmas custom, but one that broke a law which forbade that slaves be taught to read. *Photograph courtesy Janet Hobizal*

The elegant, strikingly colorful Mount Vernon dining room with its classic Paladian window was the scene of dinners mentioned in George Washington's diary. *Photograph courtesy Mount Vernon Ladies Association*

# 3.

## Colors of Christmas

**Top:** Golden yellow walls brighten the living room of The Pittock Mansion—creating a bright foil for Christmas reds and greens. *Photograph by Michael Henley/Contemporary Images, courtesy The Pittock Mansion Society*
**Above:** Sparkling metallic gold adds seasonal glamor to the regal russet table setting at Hearthside Homestead. *Photograph by Ruth A.B. Clegg/Angell Fine Arts Ltd., courtesy Hearthside Homestead*
**Opposite:** The home of noted Missouri artist George Caleb Bingham. *Photograph by Janeen Aggen, courtesy Independence, Missouri Tourism*

The traditional colors of Christmas are a brilliant red and bright green—festive primary colors that play off one another in perfect harmony. It's not necessary to ascribe religious significance (red for the blood of Christ, green for everlasting life) to thrill to their vitality. And, while they are no where legislated, red and green are *the* Christmas colors. In most historic houses these two vibrant colors show up in seasonal decorations. In early houses, they appear in evergreens, including holly with its brilliant red berries, used as sprays and garlands to decorate mantels and overdoors and for creating wreaths for windows, walls and over-mantels.

As America prepared for its Bicentennial, preservationists discovered that early houses sported much bolder, brighter colors than had been suspected. In houses of later periods, it's possible to find red and green daringly used as colors of walls. The Vaile Mansion in Independence, Missouri is a striking example.

In houses decorated with Victorian exuberance, red and green ornaments decorate trees. Red and green wraps gift packages. Red and green candles light up windows, mantels, and tabletops. Red pillows add color to chairs. Red candies and apples fill bowls. Red and green ribbons trim trees and packages. And red stockings hang at mantels.

Those Victorians who remained true to red and green as the holiday color scheme occasionally opted for variety by moving into pinky or maroon reds (and pinks) and deeper or lighter greens

Blue—in its great variety—is a favorite historic house color for walls. Compare the genteel blue of Waddesdon's Blue Dining Room with the more vivid blues of walls at Blithewold Vaile and Oldfields-Lilly. These walls are a beautiful foil for snow-white accessories and perhaps small accents of red and green.

In both early and later houses, metallic gold and silver add gleam and glamour to traditional red and green decorations. See these metals in candlesticks, bowls, trays, vases, mirror frames and sculpture. See them also in ornaments on trees. And in the Victorian era—when wall colors may be pink, aqua, **sky** blue, goldenrod yellow or some other exotic color—see gold and silver threads woven into ribbons used to trim trees and as ties for gift packages and bows on wreaths. The glow of these metals also show up in glittering ornaments for lavishly decorated trees.

Historic houses are full of ideas for decorating for the holidays. Many richer as well as poorer houses make wonderful use of nature's bounty and it's wide range of colors, including earth-toned leaves, nuts, pine cones, and bare branches. Citrus fruits introduce bright natural colors. And seashells add subtle color and texture. Sometimes, these items are displayed casually; at other times a variety of items are combined to become complex works of art. All lend their color to the holiday décor so that Christmas at Historic houses is indeed a colorful experience.

Christmas greenery
contrasts vividly
with sophisticated
shell pink walls

**Top:** Walls of the Bue Dining Room at Waddesdon create a delightful backdrop for unexpected holiday decorations in snow white. *Photograph by Mike Fear, courtesy Waddesdon Manor*

**Above:** Red poinsettias flash Christmas color against classic Adamesque blue walls and elegantly carved mantel in the Joseph Manigault House, a premier example of Federal style architecture. Photograph courtesy The Charleston Museum, Charleston, South Carolina

**Right:** A vivacious Marine blue highlights Blithewold's setting on Narragansett Bay and inspires holiday decorations that include a sailboat. *Photograph by Warren Jagger, courtesy Blithewold Mansion, Gardens & Arboretum*

A vivacious Marine blue highlights Blithewold's setting on Narragansett Bay and inspires holiday decorations...

The rose pink of walls  is echoed by rosy pink poinsettias at Butterworth Center, the home built for the granddaughter of the founder of the famed John Deere Plow Works. *Photograph by Holly Vermeire, courtesy Butterworth Center & Deere-Wiman House*

**1.**

**2.**

**3.**

1. Vaile's vivid red walls are stylishly au courant. *Photograph Janeen Aggen, courtesy Independence, Missouri Tourism*

2. A delight to holiday visitors, a unique hutch in a medley of gorgeous fall-harvest colors is a show-stopping accent in the northeast parlor of the Webb House. *Photograph by Charles T. Lyle, courtesy Webb-Deane-Stevens Museum*

3. Bold green enlivens walls in the Second Empire-style home of Harvey Vaile in Independence, Missouri. *Photograph by Janeen Aggen, courtesy Independence, Missouri Tourism*

Whimsical and striking

# *4.*

# *Stockings Hung With Care*

Clement Moore noted in his poem *Twas the Night Before Christmas* that *"the stockings were hung by the chimney with care."* Stockings—one of the many customs associated with Christmas—enliven mantels and other places in many historic houses. Whether they are simple cotton stockings in poorer houses or lavish concoctions of velvet, lace, ribbons and beads in houses from the late Victorian era, they're hung with care in a tradition of unknown origin.

The tale most often told about the original Christmas Stocking is that of the nobleman whose wife died after a long illness, leaving him with three very beautiful daughters and a depleted estate. With no money, it did not seem possible to arrange suitable marriages for the daughters. On Christmas Eve, the daughters washed their stockings and hung them at the mantel to dry. During the night, Saint Nicholas filled the stockings with gold—enough that the nobleman could arrange his daughter's' marriages and they could live happily ever afterwards!

During the years and in different parts of the world, stockings get filled with various things—tiny toys, fruits, candies—but probably not gold. According to some, naughty children's stockings get filled with coal. Of course, none of those are in historic homes!

In some families, each child has his personalized stocking that is hung on the Christmas mantel year after year, creating a tradition, making lasting memories. Probably few of the Historic Houses display stockings that actually belonged to family members, but those on display do represent the style of the interior and the taste of the family that lived there. This custom of hanging a stocking at the mantel for each member of the family is mentioned in recollections of Christmases in the White House by the late Lady Bird Johnson (see Part 1, Living Legends). She wrote in her diary: "We went upstairs to the Yellow Oval Room, where the red velvet stockings—now eight—hung from the mantel."

**Opposite:** Stockings are the focus of this mantel at the Denver mansion of the Unsinkable Molly Brown. *Photograph by Jeff Padrick/King Studios, courtesy Molly Brown Museum*
**Right:** At Vaile Mansion, an extravaganza of fancy silk stockings and flowers, tulle swags, and more reflect the Victorian unrestrained enthusiasm for all things bright and beautiful. *Photograph by Janeen Aggen, courtesy Independence, Missouri Tourism*

1. At Vaile Mansion, fancy silk stockings and flowers, tulle swags, and more reflect the Victorian love of fantasy and elegance. *Photograph by Janeen Aggen, courtesy Independence, Missouri Tourism*
2. Stockings in true Christmas red and green underscore traditional holiday décor at Blithewold. *Photograph by Warren Jagger, courtesy Blithewold Mansion, Gardens & Arboretum*
3. Apricot silk stockings accented with gilded leaves adorn the mantel at Vaile Mansion. *Photograph by Janeen Aggen, courtesy Independence, Missouri Tourism*

Whimsical red-and-white stripe stockings hang at the mantel in a room with striking red-orange-red walls in the Denver mansion of the Unsinkable Molly Brown.
*Photograph by Jeff Padrick/King Studios, courtesy Molly Brown Museum*

# 5.

## Oh Tannenabum!

Every inch of the show-stopping tree in Flagler's Great Hall is covered in beautiful ornaments. Below, gaily wrapped presents full of thrilling promise encircle the base of the enormous evergreen. *Photograph courtesy Flagler Museum*

Visitors should not expect to see Christmas trees in the authentic interiors of homes of America's Founding Fathers. They celebrated Christmas in a very low-key style and were more apt to increase the decorations for New Year's events. Visitors should be prepared to see in houses from later eras—particularly Victorian era houses—an amazing array of Christmas Trees, ranging from small tabletop gems like the one used as a dining table centerpiece at Roseland to glorious ceiling-grazing *glamazons* like the Flagler's grand hall tree.

Visitors can expect to see spectacular trees at castles such as Waddesdon, the Rothschild's breathtaking home in England (Chapter 10), and Biltmore in Ashville, North Carolina (Chapter 9), where nearly 100 Christmas trees can be seen throughout the estate. Biltmore even advises on how to decorate a Christmas Tree—*Biltmore style*. For example, if a tree is to be 14 feet high, Biltmore designers advise on planning to use 12 boxes of ornaments and 32 sets of electric lights (which should be installed first). Trees of this size are visible in many other homes of the historically rich and famous seen in *Christmas At Historic Houses*. But, in many historic homes, imaginatively decorated trees of modest sizes could fit easily into most of today's living rooms and decorating schemes. Large or small, all trees seen in homes in this book are bound to inspire.

**Opposite:** Waddesdon's Blue Dining Room. *Photographs by Mike Fear, courtesy Waddesdon*
**Below:** At Waddesdon Manor in Buckinghamshire, England, ornaments of sculpted figures echo those of nearby sculpture. *Photograph by Mike Fear, courtesy Waddesdon Manor*

Tree with faux snow on its **elegant branches**

## Christmas Tree Origins

Christmas Tree history is relatively recent; that is, the Christmas tree was not a part of the Biblical recording of the nativity. The idea of going into the field, cutting down an evergreen tree, bringing it home, then bedecking it with items totally foreign to its nature is generally traced to 16th century Germany. From that point, the story of the Christmas tree—beginning with its acceptance by the established Church as a key part of the holiday celebration—is one of continuing change.

Of course, the story of the Christmas celebration is one of change over time and location. During what is now considered The Holidays, America's founding fathers celebrated the winter season. George Washington's entries in his fascinating diary (excerpts are included in Chapter 11) show that on Christmas Day, he went about business as usual. On one Christmas Day, he attacked the Hessians. His was a fairly typical attitude among those influenced by Puritan England Mary Crowninshield left her Riversdale home to join her husband, who was Secretary of the Navy, in Washington, D.C., during the winter of 1815-1816. She wrote to her mother in Massachusetts: "Christmas morning...seems more like our Independence...I am going to the Catholic Church—it is their great day." At Mount Vernon, Monticello, Riversdale and other houses of America's early days, you will see evergreen decorations used to add color and texture to winter-weary interiors, but waste no time looking for Christmas trees. (See Mount Vernon in Chapter 11 and Monticello in Chapter 34.)

Mary Crowninshield's comment reflected the notion that the Roman Catholic Church had appropriated the pagan celebration of the winter solstice, merely putting a Christian face on a popular event, and later accepting the Christmas Tree with the same aplomb. But, as many Historic Houses attest, non-Catholics did come 'round to accepting and adopting with glee both Christmas and the Christmas tree!

Research traces the gradual spread across Europe in the early 1800s of the decorating of a Christmas tree by the well-to-do. Some cite the 1848 *Illustrated London News* image of Queen Victoria, Prince Albert and their children near their Christmas tree as popularizing the idea of Christmas as a child-focused, family-centered holiday, a decorated Christmas Tree as its symbol. Dale Wheary of Maymont Mansion in Richmond, Virginia says, "In 1850, this image was slightly altered for publication in the *Godey's Lady's Book*, a popular American periodical, and thereby, the custom achieved popularity in the United States. It's interesting to note," Wheary adds, "that the earliest recorded Christmas tree in Williamsburg was in 1842. By 1900, one in five households had a Christmas tree."

## Ornamenting The Evergreen

Dale Wheary describes the mid-19th century trees as "guileless little tabletop trees." Gilding the lily, so to speak, seems a natural inclination, for it wasn't long before evergreens trees brought indoors were embellished. At first, nature's bounty of nuts, feathers, pinecones, and berries and popcorn hand-strung into ropes were readily at hand and easily pressed into service. Wheary, "Early in the nineteenth century, Christmas trees were decorated with simple ornaments, mostly handmade and *edible*—gilded nuts, candy, and popcorn garlands.."

Ornaments appeared, hand-made and imaginatively using whatever resources were available. Some became a cultural tradition. *Papir klip* (cut paper) seen on the trees at the Petersen House in Tempe, Arizona is an excellent example. Using white or colored paper, cut into intricate, lace-like geometric patterns, *papir klip* has become a Scandinavian tradition and the woven heart a favorite recurring motif.

Paper ornaments were popular elsewhere, as well. Dr. Marcia Young, Director, says that trees at the David Davis Mansion in Bloomington, Illinois are decorated with Dresdens, "the most exquisite paper ornaments ever made." Eventually, the new color lithography made it possible to produce paper ornaments in quantities (and the Christmas cards, which quickly followed).

Dr. Young says: "The cottage industries in Germany and in the U.S., which cranked out the Dresden Victorian ornaments

Trees with themes expressed imaginatively with ornaments—tiny hatboxes, oriental fans, flags, and so on—seem to reflect design's inclination to innovate.
*Photograph courtesy Sherwood-Davidson House*

by the thousands, also produced other items that are much sought after by collectors today, including Raphael Tuck paper toys, crepe paper and scrap paper dolls...."

Another hand-made ornament seen on Scandinavian trees is a small goat-like figure crafted of straw bound in red ribbon. These figures, called Julebukk, were inspired by Viking worship of Thor and his goat. The goat eventually evolved into a devilish figure and was banned by the Church. After a suitable period, a reformed Julebukk reappeared in a less threatening guise to become a traditional ornament..

Lavishly decorated trees in houses of the Victorian Era reflect the Victorian love of excess. To the Victorians, less was never more. More was more, and ever so *much better*! Christmas trees in the Victorian style are laden with a wide assortment of items, including Oriental fans, fanciful fruits, decorative greeting cards, ropes of beads, exotic feathers, ribbon of silk, satin and velvet, and glorious glass ornaments. Dr. Young, Director of the David Davis Mansion, says that the trees there are decorated with a variety of glass figurative ornaments, and hand-blown heavy glass globes called kugels.

In some cases, an ornament inspired a tradition. At the David Davis Mansion in Bloomington, Illinois, that ornament is a green glass pickle! According to Dr. Young, each year, a gloriously green glass pickle is hidden among the branches of a great Christmas Tree. "Good luck during the coming year is promised to the fortunate finder of the lucky glass pickle," she says. To many, the idea of ornaments as family heirlooms—richly imbued with meaning and memories of annual family Christmas celebrations, with a grandly decorated tree as the heart and core of each—is a Victorian sentiment worth keeping.

In addition to all other ornaments, Victorians loved dolls and children's toys of all sorts. They decorated not only trees, but rooms throughout the house with these charming objects.

In 1880, Woolworth sold manufactured ornaments, making bright, shiny, fancy ornaments in many colors available to the masses.

Metaphorically speaking, Victorians left no stone unturned when it came to decorating a Christmas tree. And once every square inch of the Victorian Christmas tree itself has been adorned, colorful, artfully wrapped and beribboned gift boxes were piled at the foot of the tree, as they are in Flagler's Grand Hall.

Since the designer seems to lurk in every heart, in due time order was wrested from more chaotic Victorian decoration and it became fashionable to decorate trees with themes. Flag trees—proudly waving small American flags—became popular. Trees with a variety of themes, including expressive color schemes—can be seen from house to Historic House.

**Above:** Mount Vernon ornament.
**Bottom, Left:** The David Davis Mansion in Illinois, *photograph by Patricia Schley, courtesy David Davis Mansion,*
**Center:** the Sherwood-Davidson House in Ohio, *photograph courtesy Sherwood-Davidson House*
**Right:** the Physick House in New Jersey, *photograph courtesy Mid-Atlantic Center for the Arts*

Trees with PATRIOTIC themes— sporting tiny American flags — were seen in houses ACROSS THE NATION

# Electric Lights Replace Candles

*C*andles—traditionally representing Christ the Light of the World—had been used for a very long while to add magical color and light to Christmas trees. It is said that Martin Luther decorated his tree with lighted candles. A dangerous practice that imperiled homes and their occupants, the shaky practice of candle-lit trees became outmoded in 1882. Then, Edward Johnson, working with Thomas Edison, developed his idea of Christmas Lights to run on electricity. That happened at about the same time that electricity became available for residential use.

Christine Cross, a Curator of Hearthstone House in Appleton, Wisconsin notes that Hearthstone was the nation's first private residence to be lighted by a centrally located hydroelectric station! The original light switches are still used today at Hearthstone. Ms. Cross says,

> It is amazing walking into this museum and realizing that you are standing on the threshold of the use of electricity domestically. This house proved Edison right: electricity could be used safely in the home.

Prominent Midwest architect William Waters designed the house, which was built in 1881-1882 for the manager of Appleton Paper and Pulp Mill, Henry J. Rogers, and his family. It was, of course, Appleton's paper mills and their need for power to run them that prompted the interest in a hydroelectricity station. The Fox River, with its natural incline that built momentum along its stream, was a natural source of the power needed to generate electricity. So Appleton, Wisconsin (and not New York City or New Jersey, Edison's home state) was the first city in the country to build a hydroelectric station.

While it is usually the architecture and interior decorating that commands attention in any grand house, at

*The first private residence in the United States to have electric lights—Hearthstone in Appleton, Wisconsin, which was not decorated for the holidays at the time of the photograph. Photograph courtesy Hearthstone Historic House Museum*

Hearthstone, technology trumps. Science buffs will thrill at seeing the original electroliers (electric light fixtures). And the original light switches that on September 30, 1882, were thrown, lighting up Hearthstone and eventually the whole nation.

No professionally photographed interior views are available of Hearthstone's uniquely historical electric light fixtures but electric lights as Christmas Tree ornaments were a big hit. Dr. Marcia Young, Director of the David Davis Mansion in Bloomington, Illinois, says that electric light bulbs in the shape of Santa's, fruits, and flowers are part of an exhibition of authentic decorations on display at the Mansion during the holidays.

Grover Cleveland introduced electric lights to the White House in 1895. Then, only the wealthy could afford them. Dale Weary of Maymont says, "One source cites the cost at today's equivalent of $1,000 to $2,000."

## Let There Be Light—Outdoors!

*B*y 1912, it was possible to light up outdoor Christmas trees and these appeared in Boston—which once had banned Christmas! Spectacularly lit outdoor trees can be seen at Waddesdon, Oldfield-Lilly, Blithewold, Biltmore, and many other houses.

For history's creative homeowners, it was only a small leap from decorating outdoor trees to lighting up the house itself!

The logical progressive move—lighting gazebos and other garden structures.

Historic Houses vividly attest that the *decorated* Christmas tree—possible to accomplish on any budget—became an integral and spectacular part of the most celebrated of all holidays.

*Bright lights in trees and accenting the house guide visitors across a Christmas snow to beautiful Blithewold by the sea. Photograph by Warren Jagger, courtesy Blithewold Mansion, Gardens & Arboretum*

Gorgeous electric lights—
too **magical**
to be restricted to indoors—soon debuted as architectural,
then landscape ornamentation,
so that house and grounds served as beacons in the night;

sort of latter day **S**tars.

*Photographs by Hugh Palmer,
courtesy Waddesdon Manor*

# dazzling
## fairyland

**Top:** The romantic gazebo beams like glowing garden sculpture at Hearthside. *Photograph by Ruth A.B. Clegg/Angell Fine Arts Ltd., courtesy Hearthside Homestead*

**Above:** Maymount, ablaze with glowing lights, stands like a monumental beacon in the night, while grounds remain shrouded in mystery. *Photograph by Mike Weeks, courtesy Maymont Mansion*

**Left:** Outdoor lighting at Waddesdon, the Rothschild estate in the English countryside, is a design *tour de force* that transforms the garden, beautiful by day, into a dazzling fairyland at night. *Photographs by Hugh Palmer, courtesy Waddesdon Manor*

Victorian
tradition

# *Decorating with Dolls and Toys*

olls and toys have been a part of the world of children forever. Ancient in origin, we see dolls in early and late historic homes. In some houses, they are scarce, precious possessions—handmade rag dolls, sock dolls, corncob dolls and so on. In the later houses—homes of the affluent—there are collections of wonderfully costumed dolls of bisque and porcelain wearing silk and satin.

Some houses mount special exhibits of dolls at Christmas time. At the Webb-Deane-Stevens Museum (the three houses are next-door to one another) in Wethersfield, Connecticut, the Stevens House exhibits the Connecticut Colonial Dames unique collection of toys.

Andy Hahn, Director of the Campbell House Museum in St. Louis, Missouri, says: "Every year at Christmas we put together an exhibit of antique Christmas decorations and toys." In one display case are "rare French toys—a doll in a goat cart and a milkmaid." One mantel in the exhibit shows bride and groom porcelain head dolls." Toys abound throughout the house on mantels, in display cases, on shelves, and under Christmas trees.

Toys of all sorts—especially little mechanical marvels—were favorite tree decorations especially during the Victorian era. Director Hahn says that at the Campbell House Museum an annual display includes "a very traditional early Victorian tabletop Christmas tree surrounded by cast iron toy horses and buggies."

The Victorian practice of decorating Christmas trees with toys continued. Rita Heller Willey told of visiting the Campbell House in St. Louis as guest of a family friend, Mary Boerste, an employee there in the early 1900s. "When my brother, Ferd, and I were small children, we visited Mary at 1508 Locust, and Mr. Hugh [Campbell] told us to pick a toy from the Christmas tree. I still have the celluloid doll I picked and the celluloid horn my brother selected."

Dolls and toys—used to decorate trees and in room décor—capture both the heart and mind of those who visit Historic Houses during the Christmas holidays.

A wooden soldier—a favorite Christmas icon—stands guard inside the entry at Waddesdon Manor. *Photograph by Mike Fear, courtesy Waddesdon Manor*

**Opposite:** At Campbell House in Saint Louis, a special exhibit of antique toys, including cast iron horses and buggies, sets beneath a traditional early Victorian tabletop Christmas tree. *Photograph courtesy Campbell House Museum.*

1.

2.

1. A generous display of toys and gifts visible beneath a majestic tree thoroughly bedecked with a dozen or more boxes of ornaments, evokes childlike glee in all who visit Biltmore at Christmas. *Photograph used with the permission of The Biltmore Company, Asheville, North Carolina*
2. Dolls at tea create a charming miniature vignette in a child's bedroom at the David Davis Mansion. *Photograph by Patricia Schley, courtesy David Davis Mansion*
3. Christmas is a natural time for lavish displays of dolls and toys, often in children's bedrooms at historic houses. *Photographs of the Bingham-Waggoner House by Janeen Aggen, courtesy Independence, Missouri Tourism*
4. Hearthside's display of vintage style dolls and greeting cards is charmingly nostalgic. *Photograph by Ruth A.B. Clegg/Angell Fine Arts Ltd., courtesy Hearthside Homestead*

3.

4.

Rare French and other dolls are exhibited with antique toys at **Campbell House** in St. Louis. *Photographs courtesy Campbell House Museum*

# *7.*

# *Wreaths That Welcome*

Rita Heller Willey was thirteen years of age in 1922—the youngest guest at the annual Christmas Day dinner at the elegant Campbell House in St. Louis, Missouri. After dinner, the Campbells sent Rita (a young lady too old for toys plucked from the Christmas tree) home with a 5-pound tin of Busy Bee candy, an envelope containing the $5 taxi fare, and a grown-up *paper-wrapped gift*—a Christmas Wreath!

At historic houses, wreaths are everywhere. They hang as a hearty ready welcome on front doors, side doors and rear doors—not infrequently in pairs! They hang on outside shutters and against window panes, alone or accompanied by swags and garlands. They dangle from decorative lamp posts, and grace fences and gates in town and country. They adorn barns, sheds, carriage houses and sometimes carriages and sleighs.

Wreaths may have begun life as outdoor decorations, but they enliven the interiors of many Historic Houses. Indoors, they can be seen on at windows, on doors, and over mantels. Wreaths show up wherever a touch of color and texture add visual delight that contributes to the sense of holiday as a period of great expectation realized.

A spectacular wreath enlivens the pedimented doorway of the classical Gate Temple at Charleston's Joseph Manigault House garden. *Photograph courtesy of The Charleston Museum, Charleston, South Carolina*

When doors wear attention-getting Christmas colors—like the barn red at the Joel Lane House **(opposite)** and bright green at the Calvin Taylor House—wreaths need not be fancy. *Photograph by Kathleen C. Ruse, courtesy the Joel Lane House Museum. Photograph courtesy the Calvin B. Taylor House Museum*

Sign
of
Welcome

# Wreath Design and Decoration

*Thee* are three traditional elements of wreath design:

> They are almost always circular, but joining two circles to create a sort of figure eight adds interest.

> Usually they are made of evergreen boughs brought into a circular shape and fastened.

> They flaunt wide red ribbons tied in large bows and left with tails to flutter at any provocation.

That said, a good look at the myriad of wreaths hanging indoors and out at historic houses reveals a staggering variety of design, thanks largely to an incredible diversity of materials used with the basic evergreens. To say that there is a wreath to suit every taste is a modest statement; perhaps even an understatement. That is not to say that all possibilities have been realized. Some Historic Houses conduct wreath-making workshops, encouraging student visitors to consider wreaths they've seen as the jumping off point for designs of their own—using materials from the grounds and gardens of the Historic House! (See Tudor Place, Chapter 15) What could be more exciting than to know that the wreath in one's home originated at a Historic House and is made of material from that house? Such a wreath is destined—like wreaths through the years—to become a cherished memory and, if preserved, a family heirloom.

Flagler's massive iron gates are adorned with a wreath wearing a bold red ribbon that welcomes holiday visitors to this Palm Beach landmark. *Photography courtesy Flagler Museum*

The Webb House at the Webb-Deane-Stevens Museum in Connecticut places a wreath—sign of welcome—in each window. *Photographs by Charles T. Lyle, courtesy Webb-Deane-Stevens Museum*

1. At The Deane House, a simple wreath greets visitors. *Photographs by Charles T. Lyle, courtesy Webb-Deane-Stevens Museum*

2. At Bidwell in Massachusetts, a wreath—likely made of near-at-hand greens accented with home-grown pinecones—gains color from a generous ribbon of Scottish plaid, a pattern virtually synonymous with Christmas. *Photograph by Paul Rocheleau, courtesy Bidwell House Museum*

3. At the Wade House in Wisconsin, a simple wreath of encircled greenery hung on a rustic door is a symbol of respite from winter's snowy storms. *Photograph courtesy Wade House Historic Site*

**Opposite:** Greenery and a big red bow are all that is needed to add Christmas cheer to the brightly-painted carriage house door at Maymont. *Photograph by Mary Linda Mann, courtesy Maymont Mansion*

**4.**

*Look*

**3.**

**5.**

1. Double doors at the Raleigh Tavern are adorned with wreaths of mostly dried flowers accented with greenery. The transom overdoor boasts a wreath singularly offset with clay pipes and flanked with simpler wreaths. *Photographs courtesy The Colonial Williamsburg Foundation*
2.. *Faux* wreaths (and matching garlands and swags) of lifelike white pine, Douglas fir, laurel, spruce, and cedar and real pinecones can be ordered online at www.williamsburgmarketplace. com (1-800-446-9240). Add your own fruits, berries, bows or other embellishments!
3. Peanuts form a figure-8 design for the Scrivener Store Door.
4. and 5. The Peyton Randolph House door wears a fairly simple wreath in comparison to the fancy concoction of balsam fir, apples, wheat, and yarrow accented with feathers at the right.

Visiting Historic Houses

o Come! All are welcome—everyone has a standing invitation to call at Historic Houses during the Holiday Season. Join the throng, and be a part of keeping an ages-old tradition alive.

Simply accept the invitations to the public that go out in myriad ways well ahead of the Season. Look on-line, since most Historic Houses are up-to-date with electronic communications, including e-newsletters, e-mail, Facebook, Twitter, and more! Well in advance of the Season, look on-line at Historic House sites for a calendar of events. Check editorial features in the Home and Garden Section of your local newspaper. And local TV stations often "tour" the decorated House ahead of Opening Day. Check Events Calendars in newspapers, local magazines, and on-air. They list dates and hours for visiting, and mention whether there is (usually is not) a fee for visiting. Of course, the telephone is not extinct! Marking one's calendar may mean just picking up the telephone and calling the House!

VIP parties may be by invitation only. But, these are fund-raising events. And, since the House Museums want to raise funds, getting on that valuable list of supporters is probably as simple as requesting that your name be added—and writing a check! Of course, annual Memberships make it convenient to arrange early in the year—or, before a new year begins—to attend all annual events. Periodic reminders go out to Members via newsletters. Tudor Place is great about sending out periodic electronic newsletters. Perhaps all Houses do that or soon will.

Historic Houses are ideal places to take family, friends, and out-of-town houseguests during the Holidays. And since decorations and events change annually, plan to call at Historic Houses every Season.

Welcome
Home

# 8.

## Welcome Home

Liz Hart McMillan

On blue snowy eves, Yule fires and candlelight cast their spells as they lead us by warm, flickering light into the storied past of enchanting historic houses and back out again into our own futures, inspired by deeply felt traditions and treasured values we've been lucky enough to glimpse at their sources. Heroes, both everyday and grand—real people—built these very real houses, often from little more than dreams. These places in America and their people whisper to us from Christmases past about what and who we all are, whether our families arrived generations ago or are newly welcomed to America's shores and heartlands. In England, the Rothschild home reminds us of an era in which that nation fought to preserve cherished traditions.

Each year, the curators, staff, dedicated volunteers and supporting friends of these domestic museums fill them with life and wonder for the yuletide. Decorations, in keeping with the atmospheres and periods of the houses, are hung with care—inside and out. Excitement and gaiety overflow. Distinctive doors are opened wide and lantern and candlelight tours often offer us a glimpse of the special beauty of a softer, slower, gentler world before the advent of the harsher, homogenous electric light that illuminates our modern worlds of perpetual commerce and hustle-bustle. Soul-satisfying celebrations and old-fashioned festivities are planned for people to enjoy in the settings of yesteryear. We invite you to share in this through the caring words and glowing photographs of this volume.

England's historic stately homes may be diverse, but perhaps not as much so as America's historic houses, which especially in their Christmas garbs, are as diverse as her people. In this book, you will find a varied but harmonious quilt of many different styles from several centuries and periods of the homes of our forefathers and mothers. Classic 18th century elegance transformed and enlivened for the new world can be found at Thomas Jefferson's Monticello. Victorian splendor suited to our mild-mannered Mid-West makes itself at home in Indianapolis's Morris-Butler House. The rugged pioneer spirit of Texas and the particular beauty of what nature herself offers in often harsh and unexpected places is exemplified by the dignified and plain-spoken ranch of President Lyndon Baines Johnson's in Stonewall. Located across the many geographies and climates of our country, the thresholds of our historic homes are flanked by upright New England pines at Billings Farm in Vermont, by seductive magnolias in New Orleans' romantic Gallier House. Would that we could show all Historic Houses, but throughout these pages, a thrilling variety of homes surprise and inspire.

This is more than a picture book of splendid seasonal decorations amidst impressive architecture and tableaux of nostalgic moments we may all wish to emulate in our own homes.

Historic houses aren't just fine examples of scale and proportion, molding and newel posts. They also preserve the stories and dreams that imbued and drove their builders who wouldn't settle for the ordinary in any part of their lives. Christmas at Historic Houses shares some of those hopes and extraordinary accomplishments, most often from humble beginnings; it opens our hearts and minds to what makes these houses so special—their spirits. Spirits imprinted on them by the people who conceived and created them—be they modest, vernacular farmhouses with the lovely and simple integrity of Cross Creek, the 1930's Florida Everglades home of authoress Marjorie Kinnan Rawlings, who won a Pulitzer for her tender and moving novels (and who was also a terrific cook), or magnificent estates. These include North Carolina's fabled Biltmore, America's largest home (an exquisite castle, really), built by one of the legendary 19th century Vanderbilts, and the country home in England of one of the Rothschilds, a member of a preeminent European banking family.

Whatever your holiday delight, we are sure you can find it here in these remarkable dwellings. Welcome home.

**Opposite:** Karen Montee in a gown worthy of the antebellum mansion, opens the door to welcome holiday visitors to the house built by Captain Charles Richards.

# 9.

## *Biltmore Estate*

Ashville, North Carolina

### A Christmas Tradition

On Christmas Eve, 1895, George W. Vanderbilt threw open the doors to Biltmore House—welcoming for the first time visitors to his enchanting chateau in the beautiful Blue Ridge Mountains. In the banquet hall, family and friends were dazzled by the lavishly decorated, 40-foot high evergreen that graced the palatial 3,000 square foot room, with its breathtaking 70-foot-high ceiling. (To fully appreciate the size of this *room,* consider that typical American houses are 2,000 square feet or less.) This enchanting event was the beginning of what is now a singular American tradition—Christmas at Biltmore.

William Amherst Vanderbilt Cecil, who slid down the banisters of Biltmore's handsome staircases as a boy, inherited his grandfather's estate. He continues the vision for Biltmore and the zeal for celebrating Christmas. Each year, from November to January, Biltmore—*the largest private home ever built in America*—opens its magnificent doors to throngs of eager visitors. As many as 250,000 excited holiday celebrants tour 65 or more of Biltmore's 250 rooms. Visitors thrill to the opulence of a Christmas celebrated at this glorious estate on a scale unmatched anywhere else

a house covering four acres of an 8,000 **acre** estate

Biltmore, America's largest private home annually welcomes thousands of visitors to "Christmas At Biltmore." Thousands of twinkling lights add to the magic of its imposing exterior. **Opposite:** The Oak Sitting Room, where Edith Vanderbilt planned meals with the head housekeeper., thousands of twinkling lights add to the magic of its imposing façade. *Photograph used with the permission of The Biltmore Company, Asheville, North Carolina .*

dazzling
opulence

# Decorating for the Holidays

$\mathscr{P}$lanning is year 'round, for the splendidly decorated house and grounds are awe-inspiring. The sheer numbers of decorations are staggering. Over 100 evergreen trees are decorated with thousands of ornaments. A 14-foot tree, for example, requires 12 boxes of ornaments and 32 sets of lights. More than 1,000 wreaths with impressive bright red bows and 1,500 poinsettias add color indoors and out. Some 20,000 feet of garland festoons doorways, stair railings, mantels and other surface.

Inside the legendary Banquet Hall, a 35- to 40-foot high evergreen is adorned with over 500 ornaments and 500 wrapped and hanging packages.

In the Tapestry room, four 14-foot trees are each laden with 400 German blown-glass ornaments and 600 twinkling lights.

Throughout the house, hundreds of lushly embellished wreaths adorn doors, stairs—including the grand staircase with its four-story high candelier, and wherever a vibrant bit of green might add just the right decorative touch.

Indoors, miles of lights add sparkle to the spectacular scene that dazzles during the day and mesmerizes as the setting sun slips behind darkening mountains and night falls at Biltmore.

The Oak Sitting Room. Family portraits in this room are by John Singer Sargent.
*Photograph used with the permission of The Biltmore Company, Asheville, North Carolina*

The two-story high Library—his favorite room—houses 10,000 of George Vanderbilt's 23,000 volume collection of books.
*Photograph used with the permission of The Biltmore Company, Asheville, North Carolina*

On Christmas Eve 1895, guests entered this doorway when George W. Vanderbilt officially opened Biltmore House. *Photograph used with the permission of The Biltmore Company, Asheville, North Carolina*

## Evenings at Biltmore

Family and guests started their day in the first floor Breakfast Room, presided over by a portrait of Cornelius "Commodore" Vanderbilt, founder of the family fortune. *Photograph used with the permission of The Biltmore Company, Asheville, North*

*T*he Candlelight Christmas Evenings, reservation-only tours, are the only opportunity to visit interiors of Biltmore House at night. The stroll begins with a walk along luminary-lined paths that lead to the impressive entry. Inside, the house is illuminated by soft glow of fireplace and candlelight—much as it was in 1895, when George W. Vanderbilt welcomed guests into Banquet Hall. Music by choirs and instrumentalists entertain guests.

Throughout house and grounds during the holiday season, hosts share stories about holiday traditions at the palatial estate, and accomplished staff share their expertise. Floral display designers offer tips on decorating Christmas trees and interiors. Visitors learn how to design gracious centerpieces to enliven a holiday table, using natural materials from their own gardens.

At Biltmore Estate Winery—America's most-visited winery—staff members share their expertise in serving perfectly just the right wine with a particular food. These special sessions are held frequently during the holiday season.

## Bringing Biltmore Home

*S*hopping, the great American pastime, is possible at Biltmore eleven unique shops which offer fine furnishings inspired by Biltmore House, plants that carry on Biltmore's gardening legacy, and exclusive decorative accessories made especially for the estate's gift shops.

Festive meals are available in a variety of settings at the Estate's four restaurants now that Biltmore has become a Christmas destination for lovers of this special holiday.

During today's Christmas seasons, a benign seated stone lion keeps watch at the Entry, wearing a collar of greenery and a red ribbon. *Photograph used with the permission of The Biltmore Company, Asheville, North Carolina .*

The ceremonial Grand Staircase, illuminated by a four-story candelier with 72 bulbs, is heavily draped and swagged in evergreen rope and red ribbon, heightening the drama of the sweeping spiral design. *Photograph used with the permission of The Biltmore Company, Asheville, North Carolina*

# About Biltmore

*The Biltmore Estate Visit Planner* explains the origin of the estate:

Biltmore House began in George Vanderbilt's mind as a modest home on a mountain ridge. Richard Morris Hunt, one of the era's leading architects, enlarged and expanded that vision. Fortunately, his client agreed and could afford to build a house that remains the largest privately owned home in America.

Biltmore became a self-supporting country retreat where Vanderbilt and his family and friends could pursue art, literature, and horticulture.

The design of Biltmore House is based on three 16th century French châteaux. The 175,000 square foot structure sets on four acres of land. Construction began in 1889, and although the house was opened six years later, work continued for several years before Biltmore was completed. Eleven million bricks were required to build it.

The interior features a grand spiraling staircase that rises to four stories. Restoration of the fourth floor was completed and that area opened in 2006. Within its 250 rooms are 30 bedrooms and 43 bathrooms. There are 65 fireplaces to warm its imposing rooms.

The "mile-long" library holds 10,000 volumes of Vanderbilt's collection of 23,000 books. Reportedly, novelist Henry James explained (or perhaps complained) to friends that his bedroom was at least a half mile away! Then, had he lost his way, there were 30 or more servants to point him in the right direction. Today, more than that number of staff—there are 1800 employees at the estate—prepare for the thousands of touring visitors who descend upon the mansion year 'round.

For sports loving family and friends, Biltmore included an indoor swimming pool and a bowling alley. Today's guests may enjoy outdoor activities such as hiking, biking, horseback riding and raft-floating on the French Broad River.

Furnishings—large and small—and art are those originally collected by George Vanderbilt and his wife, Edith. They include paintings by French Impressionist Renoir, Whistler, and family portraits by John Singer Sargent.

Preservation and restoration are important at Biltmore, where nine 16th century Flemish tapestries, woven with golden thread, were restored by conservators in Biltmore's own facilities.

In Mrs. Edith Vanderbilt's bedroom, fabrics that greeted her arrival there as a 25-year old bride, were reproduced in France a century later, *on the same looms!*

On estate grounds there are gardens, a winery, and a farm village with animals that visiting children may pet.

Landscape architect Frederick Law Olmsted designed the grounds of the estate, which consisted originally of 125,000 acres.

Sumptuous greenery from three gardens—the formal Italian Garden, informal Shrub Garden, and ornamental Walled Garden—enrich interiors each Christmas, when Biltmore once again recreates the exuberant spirit of the very first *Christmas at Biltmore,* the best of the Gilded Age, now the most spectacular celebration in America. An admission fee helps maintain this extraordinary home that is an important, inspiring, and continuing part of America's amazing history.

During the holidays, musicians perform traditional music for the delight of visitors to the Music Room, finished in 1976, and throughout the house and grounds. *Photograph used with the permission of The Biltmore Company, Asheville, North Carolina*

*tradition continues*

The Banquet Hall—with a seven-story high ceiling—was the scene of dinner parties and holiday celebrations. In this room, on Christmas Eve 1895, the first guests to Biltmore were greeted by a 35-foot high Christmas tree—a tradition that continues. Intimate family meals were enjoyed in front of the triple-hearth fireplace. *Photograph used with the permission of The Biltmore Company, Asheville, North Carolina*

# 10.

## Waddesdon Manor

Buckinghamshire, England

### A Merry Olde Christmas

What could be merrier than Christmas in a 16th century French-style châteaux in jolly old England, especially when that châteaux is Waddesdon Manor! This magnificent structure, built at the end of the 19th century (1874-89) by Baron Ferdinand de Rothschild, is furnished with his inspired collection—a glorious gathering of the finest in decorative arts in what interior designers call *le style Rothschild*.

At Christmas time, lavish seasonal decorations transform an already magical place into a stunning wonderland. Outside, the grounds, like the house, are treated to all the decorative trimmings of the holiday season. All is merry and bright, and at night a mere glimpse of the lavishly lit châeaux is enough to lift the spirits of the most dour.

Indoors, a different theme each year—a Hans Christian Andersen fairy tale or some other—inspires both the Christmas decorations and celebratory events. The annual theme—appealing to the child in everyone—can be found on-line at Waddesdon.org well before the holiday season.

Waddesdon has always welcomed children. During his lifetime, Baron Ferdinand organized annual treats for children and their parents from surrounding villages. During WW II, James and Dorothy de Rothschild opened Waddesdon's doors to house hundreds of children under age five who were evacuated from London. On Christmas Day, there was a lighted Christmas tree and gifts, and Mrs. de Rothschild is said to have declared, "the house never looked so attractive." These days, children can greet a costumed Father Christmas as he walks around the Gardens during December weekends. And, they may write and post their letters to Father Christmas on the walls of the Power House, ready for Christmas Eve,

Events abound. One of the most popular of many throughout the holidays is the Christmas Fair and Food Market, where decorations, handmade candies, wreaths and garlands are for sale. For gourmands and foodies, advanced reservations may be made for lunchtime or evening Christmas parties featuring Christmas foods once served in the Manor. The Events Team can arrange exclusive access tours of The Rothschild Collection, entertainment by a musical band or magicians, and wine tastings with the Master of Wine. Unique Rothschild Wine gifts can be designed.

Ornamented ornamental, and trees in tubs **brighten** the entry portico.

*Photograph by Barry Keen, courtesy Waddesdon Manor*

mystical
fairytale

## Waddesdon's Care and Keep

*H*oliday host at Waddesdon is the National Trust, to whom Waddesdon was bequeathed by James de Rothschild, whose widow, Dolly, continued to manage the house until her death in 1988. James, a member of the French arm of the great banking family and her great-nephew, had inherited Waddesdon at the death of Miss Alice (who inherited the house in 1898, at the death of her brother Ferdinand, who built Waddesdon). In 1957, in order to ensure its existence in perpetuity, Waddesdon was bequeathed to the National Trust.

The Rothschild family maintains an active interest in the running of Waddesdon through a family charitable trust under the chairmanship of Lord Rothschild. Since taking over responsibility for the Manor, he has masterminded an extensive program of building and restoration work. The Manor—closed to the public for almost four years in order for the most disruptive work to take place—reopened in 1994, but the challenging program continues.

At Christmas time, thousands of tiny points of light play across the façade of Waddesdon, adding to the mystical quality of its fairy tale architecture that brings 18th Century France to the English countryside. An enormous illuminated tree shields the entry. *Photograph by Barry Keen, courtesy Waddesdon Manor*

1 through 5. East Gallery may be decorated with silver ornaments one season and gold, the next. *Photographs by Mike Fear, courtesy Waddesdon Manor*

1. The charming *lit d'alcove bed* in the Blue Boudoir very practically leaves ample floorspace for a festive Christmas tree and gift-wrapping. *Photograph by Mike Fear, courtesy Waddesdon Manor*

2. The Billiards Room with its bright red rug and fresh green felt table top that seem tailor-made for the season, boasts two Christmas trees. *Photograph by Mike Fear, courtesy Waddesdon Manor*

3. A collection of antique toys—reminders, perhaps, that London children were sheltered safely here during World War II—and a Christmas tree decorated in red add a festive note to the Red Ante Room.

**Opposite:** The dramatic Red Ante Room is a brilliant foil for the White Drawing Room. Oil paintings on these and walls throughout the house form a much-lauded collection by Baron de Rothschild. *Photograph by Barry Keen, courtesy Waddesdon Manor*

# A Brief History

ℬaron Ferdinand, a member of the Austrian branch of the Rothschild family, was born in Paris and spent most of his childhood in Frankfurt and Vienna. From his English mother, Ferdinand learned to love the English countryside, and when she died, he decided to live in England. There, he fell in love with his first cousin Evelina, an English Rothschild. They were married in 1865. Sadly, after eighteen months of marriage, Evelina and their baby died in childbirth. His youngest sister, Alice (always called Miss Alice), came from Europe to be a companion to Ferdinand, who threw himself into collecting 18th century art.

In addition to his London (winter) residence, Ferdinand wanted a country house where he could entertain family and friends in season. Funds bequeathed at his father's death in 1874, permitted Ferdinand to realize plans he had formulated with Evelina. He bought the Waddesdon and Winchendon estates, consisting of 2,500 acres, from the Duke of Marlborough. A tour of ancient châteaux in France had influenced Ferdinand to build in the French Renaissance style, so he choose French architect Gabriel-Hippolyte Destailleur to design Waddesdon Manor. He hired French landscape gardener Elie Lainé to design the terraces and principal roads, and to supervise the planting of mature trees.

Some of the interior architectural elements came from structures in France. For example, oak paneling for the Breakfast Room and the Low White Room was purchased from a great-nephew of Cardinal Richelieu. Rococo paneling in the Grey Drawing Room came from a house in Paris, and the paneling in the Tower Drawing Room is Louis XVI. An East Gallery chimney piece came from a Paris post office.

Ferdinand furnished his grand house with Savonnerie carpets, Sevres porcelain, and his collection of French furniture of royal provenance, the most important outside France. Among a vast catalogue of notable paintings are Gainsborough's "Pink Boy," Watteau's "Harlequin, Pierrot and Scapin," Ruben's "Garden of Love," and works by master Dutch and Flemish artists. A George III silver service displayed in the White Drawing Room is one of only a handful of royal, neo-classical services to have survived anywhere in the world, according to Philippa Glanville, Academic Director at Waddesdon Manor (in her April 2003 article for *Apollo Magazine*). Ferdinand added to his fine furnishings collection his entire life, as did James, who inherited a substantial part of his father Baron Edmond's great collection.

Swagged ropes of evergreen—accented with berries on one occasion, dried fruit on another are a favorite decoration for the dining table set for the holiday in the White Drawing Room. *Photograph above by Barry Keen, and opposite by Mike Fear, courtesy Waddesdon Manor*

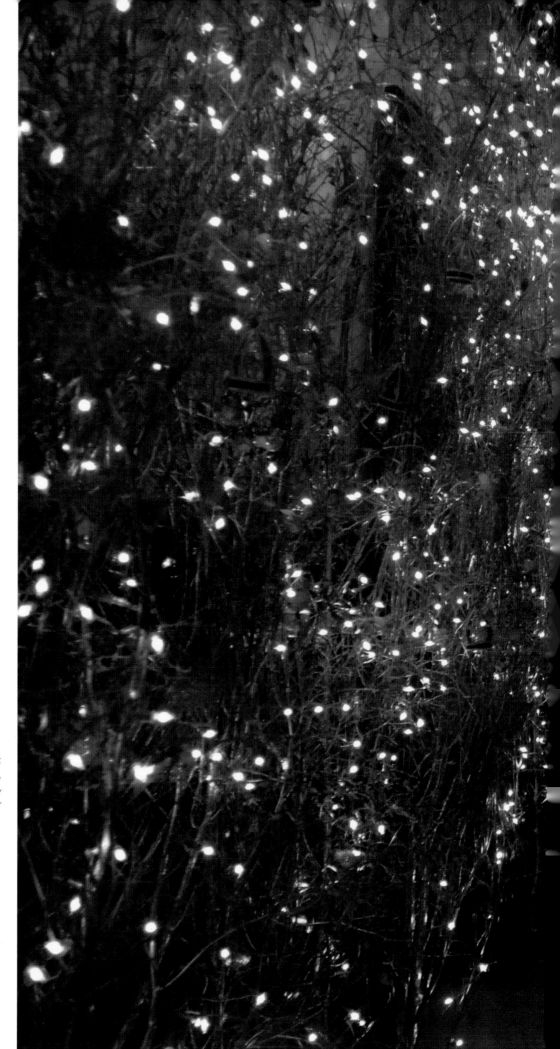

Bunched bare branches and gazillions of tiny sparkling lights create a sensation in the Kitchen Corridor. *Photograph by Barry Keen, courtesy Waddesdon Manor*

## Visiting Royals

*V*isitors to Waddesdon were the most dazzling personages of the day. In May 1890, Queen Victoria accepted an invitation (which some say she arranged) to visit. Reportedly, the Queen—most enthralled with the electricity—spent ten minutes turning a light switch on and off. Ferdinand was "delighted that the visit (preceded by many consultations with Princess Louise regarding the preferences of Her Majesty) had passed off so satisfactorily." The Prince of Wales was a regular visitor. Luminaries from all walks of life came to Waddesdon. Among them, Churchill, Curzon, Asquith, Guy de Maupassant, Anthony Trollope, and Henry James. Still, the most memorable visit—without a doubt—remains the May 1890 visit by Queen Victoria, who for thirty years preceding that visit had lived in great privacy.

Queen Victoria walked through these doors in 1890, when she accepted Baron de Rothschild's invitation to lunch. Annually, some 300,000 visitors pass through these heavily carved doors to view the same treasures that enthralled the Queen of England. *Photograph by Mike Fear, courtesy Waddesdon Manor*

Waddesdon's Blue Dining Room, with its beautifully carved, paneled walls in the French style, boasts an intriguing chandelier and a tree with *faux* snow on its elegant branches. *Photographs by Mike Fear, courtesy Waddesdon*

# Christmas in the Garden

*D*uring the Holidays, choirs perform in the Garden. In the garden is a rare example of a working Aviary housed in a historic rococo style building. Replete with an impressive collection of exotic birds, the Aviary is a principal feature today, just as it was in Ferdinand's day.

The Entrance Hall is treated to ropes and wreaths of evergreen, while trusty Wellington boots stand at-the-ready. *Photograph by Mike Fear, courtesy Waddesdon Manor.*

The Blue Dining Room, brightened only by the extraordinary chandelier and lights from the Christmas Tree. *Photographs by Hugh Palmer, above, and Barry Keene, right, courtesy Waddesdon Manor*

# *11.*

## *Mount Vernon*

Mount Vernon, Virginia

### Christmas At The First President's Home

Mount Vernon, home of the first President of the United States of America, is open every day, including Christmas Day and New year's Day, due to the efforts of the Mount Vernon Ladies' Association.

Forty-five acres of the estate—landscaped by Washington himself—are open to the public. Thirteen trees planted by Washington remain—living witnesses to his lifetime. Four gardens are filled with heirloom plants that were known to have been at Mount Vernon in the 1700s.

From the mansion's piazza there is a spectacular view of the Potomac River. Inside the historic house, an original building, rooms are filled with 18th-century treasures. Many were owned by Washington. One of the most notable items is the key to the Bastille, the infamous French prison, presented to Washington by the Marquis de Lafayette.

During the Christmas holidays, visitors to Mount Vernon may tour the mansion by candlelight, see the rarely-seen third floor to which Mrs. Washington retreated after President Washington's death, and learn much about how the nation's first First Family enjoyed Christmas there.

The Christmases of George Washington at Mount Vernon and other places during the Revolutionary War and his presidency are recorded in Washington's diaries and various writings. Mary V. Thompson, Research Specialist at Mount Vernon Estate & Gardens compiled fascinating notes about the holidays for an unpublished paper which she prepared for the Mount Vernon Ladies' Association. Activities seems almost ordinary, and that's partly what makes Mary's notes fascinating reading. They reveal, for example, Washington at times alone, at other times receiving family and friends. On some Christmas Days, he went to church; on others he played cards. Like other families, the Washingtons endured sickness during some holidays. And, faced wartime privation. And during one Christmas, Washington was aggravated by the presence of an unwelcome oyster man fishing without invitation, unintimidated by Washington and unmoved by the request that he leave. Here are Mary's extensive notes that take the reader back in time, offering glimpses of the life of the master of Mount Vernon:

**Near Right:** Evergreen branches and berries were natural seasonal decorations for over-doors, mantels, and tabletop during America's early days in which Christmas was treated much the same as any other day. *Photograph courtesy The Mount Vernon Ladies Association.*
**Opposite:** The Dining Room with its classic Paladian-style window and boldly colored walls was the setting for dinners with family and distinguished friends—many noted in George Washington's diary. *Photograph by Mark Finkenstaedt, courtesy The Mount Vernon Ladies Association*

Mount Vernon—George Washington's beloved home at his Virginia estate—with its distinctive flanking dependencies in the neoclassical style where Christmas was celebrated with none of the fanfare of the later Victorian period. *Photograph courtesy The Mount Vernon Ladies Association*

# Christmas 1758

**Saturday, 12/30/1758:** In Williamsburg; wrote letters.

**Saturday, 1/6/1759:** Married Martha Dandridge Custis—young widow with two children, at her home in New Kent County, Virginia. Her son, John Parke Custis (Jacky), was four years old; his sister, Martha Parke Custis (Patsy), was two. The new family came home to Mount Vernon in April of 1759.

# Christmas 1759

The family's first holiday season together at Mt. Vernon.

**Tuesday, 1/1/1760:** Martha Washington broke out with measles; George Washington rode around his plantation; Mrs. Barnes, a distant relative, came to visit M.W.

**Wednesday, 1/2/1760:** G.W. at home, putting papers in order; Mrs. Barnes returned home.

**Thursday, 1/3/1760:** Bad weather, G.W. at home; several slaves down with measles; G.W. hauling the seine to catch fish, but bothered by *"an Oyste[r] Man who had lain at my Landing and plagud [sic] me a good deal by his disorderly behaviour."*

**Friday, 1/4/1760:** rainy and warm; G.W. stayed home; M.W. very sick and he wrote the Reverend Mr. Green to see her in a medical capacity.

**Saturday, 1/5/1760:** M.W. better; Mr. Green came to see her and prescribed a medication; Mrs. George William Fairfax (Sally), Mr. Green, Capt. Walter Stuart, and Dr. Laurie for dinner; Mrs. Fairfax left afterward in the chariot.

**Sunday, 1/6/1760:** "The Chariot not returng. time enought [sic] from Colo. Fairfax's we were prevented from Church."; M.W. better; *"the Oyster Man still continuing his Disorderly behavior at my Landing I was obligd [sic] in the most preemptory manner to order him and his Compy. away which he did not Incline to obey till next morning."*

# Christmas 1768

(At Mount Vernon)

**Saturday, 12/24/1768:** GW rode to the mill and Dogue Run.

**Sunday, 12/25/1768:** At home all day; *"gave my overseer Morris 1.10.0; gave Mike ten shillings."*

# Christmas 1769

(Enroute to Mount Vernon after the close of the meeting of the House of Burgesses. Christmas day was spent in Fredericksburg, at Kenmore, the home of George Washington's sister, Betty Lewis, and her husband, and a visit was paid to Washington's mother. The family arrived back at Mount Vernon in time for dinner on the 28th.)

**Sunday, 12/24/1769:** Went to prayers; dined afterwards at Colonel Lewis's.

**Monday, 12/25/1769:** Dined and spent the evening at Colonel Lewis's; played cards.

# Christmas 1770

**Monday, 12/24/1770:** G.W. rode to the mill, twice.

**Tuesday, 12/25/1770:** Pohick Church and home to dinner.

# Christmas 1771

**Tuesday, 12/24/1771:** G.W. at home all day and doing paperwork; no guests.

**Wednesday, 12/25/1771:** Pohick Church with Mrs. Washington; returned to dinner.

**Saturday, 12/28/1771:** hunting; dinner at home with guests—two Mr. Tripletts, Mr. Manley, Mr. Peake, young Frans Adams, Stone Street, Mr. Peake's daughter, and Miss Fanny Eldridge.

# Christmas 1772

**Thursday, 12/24/1772:** at home all day.

**Friday, 12/25/1772:** Pohick Church; returned to dinner; Mr. Tilghman was there.

# Christmas 1773

(At Mount Verno) A bitter-sweet Christmas. Martha Washington's daughter, Patsy, had died earlier in the year and her son was planning to marry Eleanor Calvert within a month. According to the staff at the *Washington Papers*, the following incident related by artist Charles Willson Peale probably occurred during the Christmas at Mount Vernon: *"One afternoon several young gentlemen, visiters [sic] at Mount Vernon, and myself were engaged in pitching the bar, one of the athletic sports common in those days, when suddenly the colonel [George Washington] appeared among us. He requested to be shown the pegs that marked the bounds of our efforts; then, smiling, and without putting off his coat, held out his hand for the missile. No sooner...did the heavy iron bar feel the grasp of his mighty hand than it lost the power of gravitation, and whizzed through the air, striking the ground far, very far, beyond our utmost limits. We were indeed amazed, as we stood around, all stripped to the buff, with shirt sleeves rolled up, and having thought ourselves very clever fellows, while the colonel, on retiring, pleasantly observed, 'When you beat my pit*ch, young gentlemen, I'll try again'."

**Friday, 12/24/1773:** at home all day; Dr. Craik came.

**Saturday, 12/25/1773:** at home all day; Dr. Craik left after breakfast.

# Christmas 1774

**Saturday, 12/24/1774:** at home all day; guests--Richard Washington and Mrs. Newman for dinner.

**Sunday, 12/25/1774:** at home all day; guests.

# Christmas 1775

(First Christmas of the Revolution; George Washington was with the army at Cambridge, Massachusetts. Martha Washington had planned to spend that Christmas with her sister, but upon her husband's invitation, came to his quarters at Cambridge for the winter with her son and daughter-in-law. Mount Vernon suffered very cold weather and the river was blocked up; one of the servants wounded "in a playing frolic" in Alexandria on Christmas Eve and later died.)

**Sunday, 12/24/1775:** George Washington did correspondence.

**Monday, 12/25/1775 – Saturday, 1/6/1776:** wrote letters and orders.

# Christmas 1783

In November, George Washington received news that the peace treaty had been signed and the war was over. Martha Washington returned to Mount Vernon at that time. Her daughter-in-law, Eleanor Calvert Custis, was planning to marry Dr. David Stuart. The two oldest Custis granddaughters continued to live with their mother, while their younger sister, Eleanor Parke Custis (Nelly), and their brother, George Washington Parke Custis, lived at Mount Vernon and were raised by the Washingtons.

**Monday, 12/22/1783:** The governor of Maryland gave a ball at the State House in Annapolis, where the United States Congress was meeting. According to one man who was there, *"The General danced every set, that all the ladies might have the pleasure of dancing with him, or as it has since been handsomely expressed, get a touch of him."*

**Tuesday, 12/23/1783:** George Washington appeared before Congress at noon to resign his commission from the army. He and his aides left immediately for Mount Vernon and probably spent the night at a tavern along the road.

**Wednesday, 12/24/1783:** George Washington arrived home to Mount Vernon. In a letter written on Christmas Day, James Tilton said that Washington had been *"intent upon eating his Christmas dinner at home"*. Both George Mason and a Miss Lewis (probably one of the daughters of GW's sister, Betty, and her husband, Fielding Lewis) were at Mount Vernon that Christmas. (See Pamela C. Copeland and Richard K. MacMaster, *The Five George Masons: Patriots and Planters of Virginia and Maryland*, Charlottesville, Virginia, Published for the Board of Regents of Gunston Hall by the University Press of Virginia, 1975.)

# Christmas 1785

**Saturday, 12/24/1785:** Washington took care of correspondence; otherwise nothing going on; slaves "cutting wood for Christmas" in order to supply the mansion fireplaces while they were off; snowing.

**Sunday, 12/25/1785:** guests--Count Castiglioni, Colonel Burges Ball, and Mr. William Hunter to dinner; Hunter left; G.W. worked on accounts.

## Christmas 1786

**Saturday, 12/23/1786:** GW was at home at Mount Vernon all day-working; nephew Bushrod Washington and wife there; 1 cart "at the house for provision &c for Christmas" to supply the mansion house during the time the slaves were off for the holiday.

**Sunday, 12/24/1786:** At home all day; Miss Allan and Martha Washington's 3 granddaughters, Betsy, Patsy, and Nelly Custis came from their mother's home, where Nelly had been visiting, to dinner at Mount Vernon; Bushrod Washington and wife left.

**Monday, 12/25/1786:** At home all day; George Washington doing correspondence; company; Mount Vernon slaves were off.

## Christmas 1787

(At Mount Vernon with family and friends)

**Monday, 4/23/1787:** agreed to hire gardener Philip Bates or Bater; part of the contract stipulated that the gardener was to receive *"four Dollars at Christmas, with which he may be drunk 4 days and 4 nights...."*

**Saturday, 12/22/1787:** G.W. foxhunting in the morning with Colonel Humphreys, Major Washington, and Mr. Lear; later he worked; Mrs. Stuart, her four children, and Mr. George Calvert came in the afternoon.

**Sunday, 12/23/1787:** at home all day.

**Monday, 12/24/1787:** George Washington working; gave fifteen shillings to the servants *"for Christmas"*; a Mr. Snow arrived.

**Tuesday, 12/25/1787:** G.W. wrote letters.

**Wednesday, 12/26/1787:** Mr. Snow went back to Alexandria; Colonel Humphreys, *"the Gentlemen of the Family & myself went out with the hounds"*; nephews George Steptoe Washington and Lawrence Augustine Washington arrived.

## Christmas 1788

**Wednesday, 10/1/1788:** advanced twelve shillings to gardener Philip Bates *"part of his Christmas money"*.

**Saturday, 12/20/1788:** G.W. sent his carriage to Dumfries for Mrs. Washington of Bushfield and several other people.

**Sunday, 12/21/1788:** William Craik and a Washington cousin came for dinner but left afterwards; weather very cold.

**Monday, 12/22/1788:** carriage returned without the Bushfield people, possibly put off by the very cold weather; Mr. Stuart had dinner at Mount Vernon and left afterwards.

**Tuesday, 12/23/1788:** at home all day; very cold weather; it snowed.

**Wednesday, 12/24/1788:** at home all day; 4" of snow; very cold.

**Thursday, 12/25/1788:** at home; very cold weather; G.W. *"gave three shillings each to the Taylor, Shoemaker & Dutchman, six shillings each to Peter and Giles, and twelve shillings to Tobias Lear."*

## Christmas 1789

(First Christmas as President; in New York City)

**Thursday, 12/24/1789:** George Washington attending to business and writing a letter; had appointment with General Knox, the Secretary of War.

**Friday, 12/25/1789:** attended church in the morning at St. Paul's; "respectable" visitors came in the afternoon to see Mrs. Washington (note-this was her regular levee day).

## Christmas 1790

(in New York)

**Friday, 12/24/1790:** Mrs. Washington paid $10 for 2 tickets in the New York and Massachusetts Lottery for either her former daughter-in-law, Mrs. Stuart, or Mrs. Warner Washington.

**Saturday, 12/25/1790:** Mount Vernon slaves off for Christmas.

## Christmas 1791

(The Washingtons were in Philadelphia, the new seat of government.)

Sunday, 12/25, 26, 27: George Washington writing letters.

## Christmas 1792

(In Philadelphia)

**Tuesday, 12/25/1792:** George Washington working on correspondence.

## Christmas 1795

(In Philadelphia; Martha Washington's granddaughter, Nelly Custis, was spending the winter in Virginia with her mother)

**Thursday, 12/24/1795:** the Washingtons had their regular Thursday dinner for members of Congress; George Washington wrote letters.

**Friday, 12/25/1795:** According to Martha Washington, "we have spent our christmas at home as we always have done..."; George Washington writing letters.

**Monday, 12/28/1795:** Washington noted that he gave $5 to the watchmen "*as a Christmas gift*".

## Christmas 1797

(George Washington had retired from the presidency and was back at Mount Vernon. His nephew Lawrence Lewis, a young widower, joined the household late in the year.)

**Sunday, 12/24/1797:** weather calm and cold.

**Monday, 12/25/1797:** appearance of snow, but it cleared; Martha Washington's nephew, William Dandridge came; Washington worked on his accounts and wrote letter.

## Christmas 1798

At Mount Vernon

**Monday, 12/24/1798:** driving snow; Dr. Craik came to dinner; Judge Cushing and his wife, Mr. Silas Dinsmoor, and another man came in the afternoon.

**Tuesday, 12/25/1798:** weather clear; General Pinckney, his wife and their daughter came to dinner and a Captain John Spotswood came in the afternoon; George Washington writing letters; in one to George Washington Lafayette, he announced Nelly's upcoming marriage to Lawrence Lewis, which was to take place on February 22, 1799, George Washington's 67th birthday.

Granddaughter Nelly Custis was at Hope Park with her mother. Nelly's fiance, Lawrence Lewis, and her brother, George Washington Parke Custis, were "beyond the Mountains." With the young people away, George and Martha Washington had a relatively quiet Christmas, the last they would spend together. George Washington died eleven days before Christmas of 1799.

Note: Diary entries furnished by Mary V. Thompson, Curatorial Registrar, Mount Vernon Ladies' Association, Mount Vernon, Virginia. (Unpublished paper dated December, 1990; revised 5/28/1996, 11/16 & 20/2001, 11/27/2002, & 12/18/2002).

*A dream realized*

# 12.

## Blithewold Mansion

Bristol, Rhode Island

### A Blithe Christmas

*December 16, 1895*

*My dear Marjorie,*

*Tonight I expect to go to Bristol, but I do not go till midnight…I am very anxious to get the first glimpse of our new country home, that we will all love so much.
I wish you were going with me….*

*Your loving father,*

*A.S. Van Wickle*

**Below:** Blithewold, a 45-room English Country Manor style house, nestles into its ideal Christmas setting. *Photograph courtesy Blithewold Mansion Gardens & Arboretum.*
**Opposite:** The 18-foot high Blithewold tree—decked out each year in ornaments befitting a unique theme—welcomes visitors in the Great Entry Hall. *Photo by Warren Jagger Photo. Photograph courtesy of Blithewold Mansion Gardens & Arboretum.*

elegant and feminine

Blithewold, built as a summer-by-the-sea country home is a dream realized. At Christmas time, this beautiful 45-room English Country House-style mansion and its 33 acres of magnificent gardens overlooking Narragansett Bay at Bristol, Rhode Island, are a lavish fantasy come to life; and a well-established holiday tradition. Beginning well before "opening day," staff and a bevy of volunteers work 'round the clock to create the magic. Thousands come calling to revel in the beauty that is Blithewold.

Each year in the gracious entry hall, visitors are greeted by a dazzling 18-20 foot high Christmas tree swathed head-to-toe in decorations. This tree and a dozen or more throughout the house are decorated with ornaments and items that express the special theme chosen for that particular Season. Themes are always based on the vibrant lives of former owners Bessie Van Wickle McKee and her two daughters, Marjorie Van Wickle Lyon and Augustine Van Wickle Shaw. Each is visually arresting and memorable. One year, the theme featured the *Blithewold Belles*—dolls from just one of Blithewold's extraordinary collections of historic artifacts. *Letters from Paris*, was based on 19-year-old Marjorie's 1903 European tour. *Winter Solstice* was about the family's winter activities. The 2003 theme, *And Heaven and Nature Sing*" focused on music and bounty from the amazing gardens at Blithewold. Indoor Christmas trees were covered with dried flowers, gilded leaves, berries, seed pods, pinecones, and feathers, and an outdoor tree decorated with garlands of nuts and popcorns attracted winter birds.

In 2006, *Silver Bells,* was the theme and the 18-foot high Christmas tree in the grand entrance hall was covered head-to-toe with silver bells, crystal drops, pinecones covered with *faux* snow, thousands of tiny twinkling white lights, and splendid silver and red ribbon. In addition to the entrance Christmas tree, 14 professionally designed trees throughout the mansion displayed various kinds of bells—all ready to ring-in the season.

Each year, at a special Christmas Preview party, new themes are announced. Volunteer designers, many with a background in exhibit design—bring ingenuity and talent to bear, so that each new season's trees and all other decorations seem to top the previous year's extravaganza, keeping an appreciative public eagerly anticipating the moment when doors will open on Christmas at Blithewold.

Entertainment—often history in its most delightful form—abounds at Blithewold in all seasons. But the Christmas calendar is especially full. There may be a gala four-course dinner for a private party (with a theme, of course), numerous teas, readings, a series of musical performances, caroling, workshops and wreath-making classes. Specially mounted exhibitions, displays, and decorations—not merely visually exciting but engagingly informative—may include fashion and dinnerware (there are 30 sets in the butler's pantry!).

Blithewold's history is rich and long. A charming account (*Blithewold Mansion, Gardens & Arboretum, A history of the estate and the family who created it*) by Margaret Whitehead and Julie Morris, published by Save Blithewold, Inc., in 2004, is both history and guide and is available at Blithewold for $5.00. Historic highlights, based on their booklet recount that the grand house overlooking Narragansett Bay near Bristol, was built by coal baron, Augustus Van Wickle and his wife Bessie, the daughter of a coal baron. They built Blithewold as their summer retreat by the sea—a place that seemed a world away from their home in Hazelton, Pennsylvania. The setting was ideal for Augustus, who loved yachting. It offered Bessie, who loved horticulture, acreage for creating a garden..

When it was completed, the 33 acre estate consisted of the mansion, stables, guest house, tennis court, golf course, a large dock areas for the couple's 72-foot steamer yacht, a delightful sandy beach, and bathhouses. Oh yes, and Bessie's beloved gardens—a life-long passion shared by Bessie's daughter Marjorie—were begun.

The first Blithewold—a shingled Queen Anne style mansion—was completed in 1896. The couple and their eleven year-old daughter, Marjorie, was welcomed into the social life of Bristol, a town steeped in history and full of old-world charm. (Today, there are ten museums and numerous eclectic shops and fine restaurants!).

In Estelle's Room, in the elegant, very feminine Victorian manner, pink roses adorn the beautiful tree that stands near a table draped in a lace-enriched cloth. Both this table and the child's table nearby are set for tea—a favorite Victorian social custom that is observed at Blithewold during the holidays. *Photograph by Warren Jagger, courtesy of Blithewold Mansion Gardens & Arboretum.*

simplicity

Sadly, two years later, while Bessie was packing to depart Hazelton to spend the summer in Blithewold, Augustus was killed in a skeet-shooting accident. Bessie was left to deliver alone, five months later, their second daughter, Augustine.

In 1901, Bessie married William Leander McKee of Boston. The family resided on Commonwealth Avenue in Boston, but stayed at Blithewold from May until November. They often returned for Thanksgiving and Christmas holidays.

In June, 1906, the shingle-style house burned to the ground. Just a year later, a new Blithewold was built—a 45-room mansion made of stone in the English Country Manor style, designed by architects Kilham and Hopkins of Boston.

But dark days arrived in the form of the 1930s stock market crash. The McKees sold their Boston house and made Blithewold their year-round home. When Bessie, who outlived Mr. McKee, died in 1936, she left Blithewold to her daughters, Marjorie and Augustine. Marjorie, who, like her mother, loved horticulture, bought her sister's share, but Augustine continued to summer at Blithewold.

When Marjorie died at age 93 in 1976, she left the estate and funds for its upkeep to the Heritage Foundation of Rhode Island. Blithewold opened to the public in 1978. "Save Blithewold, Inc.," a group formed in 1998 when Marjorie's funds were exhausted, manages the estate. Focus is on historic preservation and horticultural excellence begun by Bessie Pardee Van Wickle McKee, who wrote in 1910:

> In improving the property the plan was to create a park with distinctive features, using the house as a centre. Everywhere nature's bounteous gifts have served, under man's skillful guidance, to create an estate in which new beauties are constantly revealed, and the perfect accord between architecture and grounds is ever apparent.

Focus—still on Blithewold's incredibly beautiful gardens—is necessarily also on raising funds needed to maintain this outstanding bit of American history. *Christmas at Blithewold* is an annual opportunity for all who wish to do so to share in a most delightful way in perpetuating this living legacy.

This mantel is decorated with great simplicity with a green garland and gold ribbon. *Photograph by Warren Jagger, courtesy of Blithewold Mansion Gardens & Arboretum.*

91

**Left:** Choralier figurines combined with greenery create a charming tableau on the sofa/library table. Wall sconces covered in evergreens take on the shape of Christmas trees. And the Austrian blinds are treated to red bows. *Photograph by Warren Jagger, courtesy of Blithewold Mansion Gardens & Arboretum.*

**Above:** In the Dining Room, white decorations contrast elegantly with rich, dark paneling. Tabletop trees flanking the fireplace mantel are highlighted with white ornamentation, repeated in swags and ribbons adorning the chairs. *Photograph by Warren Jagger, courtesy of Blithewold Mansion Gardens & Arboretum.*

# 13.

## Colonial Williamsburg

### An Original Village Christmas

Christmas begins with a bang in the historic village of Williamsburg. For 81 years, Williamsburg was the leading city in Virginia, America's most affluent colony. It was home to such patriots as George Washington, George Mason, and Peyton Randolph, whose ideals and courage created America's unique democratic system. The Reverend Dr. W.A.R. Goodwin, rector of Bruton Parrish Church, and John D. Rockefeller, Jr.—men of vision and resolve—rescued from certain oblivion Virginia's first capital in a massive preservation project that began in 1926. Mr. Rockefeller continued to be personally involved until his death in 1960.

Today, Williamsburg is America's "living history" town, home to many historic houses, and it celebrates Christmas in capital style. The Yuletide season starts on the first Sunday in December, with an evening of musical performances on several stages throughout the Historic area, followed by spectacular fireworks known as the Grand Illumination.

Throughout December, candles shine from windows of shops and homes. Evergreen wreaths, ropes, and swags adorn doorways and windows of shops and historic homes such as the Peyton Randolph House at the corner of Market Square and Nicholson Street.

Indoors, similar wreaths, ropes and swags fill homes and shops with their rich fragrance. Like those made by early colonists, these traditional handmade decorations are made of boxwood and bayberry, ingenious embellishments of shells, pine cones, and colorful fruits including (for the rich) pomegranates, pineapples and apples. They add color to windows, mantels, and stairways. Today, gift shops offer plenty of "ready-mades" for visitors to bring home, and workshops for learning how to make wreaths.

Inside historic houses, tea tables and dining tables are beautifully set for festive gatherings that focus on the traditional foods of the season. In sociable Virginia, sharing meals was an important part of holiday gatherings. Among desserts, mincemeat pie was a favorite. It was also a labor-intensive effort for colonial cooks who chopped, diced and mixed imported

Early Virginian's decorated with fresh fruits (often costly) and greenery (typically boxwood). A pineapple—an early symbol of hospitality—surrounded by stacked green apples forms this centerpiece in the Dining Room of the Governor's Palace. *Photograph courtesy of The Colonial Williamsburg Foundation.*

**Opposite:** The Governor's Palace—reconstructed in 1934 on its original foundation—was home to seven royal governors. The State of Virginia's first two governors, Patrick Henry and Thomas Jefferson also resided here. At Christmas, the Palace is bedecked with glowing candles and Christmas finery for *Grand Illumination*—the night of lights and fireworks that welcomes the season known far and wide as "Christmas at Williamsburg." *Photograph courtesy The Colonial Williamsburg Foundation.*

Williamsburg at Christmas

**Below:** This house on Nicholson Street—an original Colonial Williamsburg house—was home to Peyton Randolph, the Speaker of the House of Burgesses and President of both the First and Second Continental Congress. *Photograph courtesy The Colonial Williamsburg Foundation*

**Right:** An abundance of dishes typical of the period and the season create a welcoming sight in the Dining Room of the Peyton-Randolph house. *Photograph courtesy The Colonial Williamsburg Foundation*

fruits (largely apples and raisins) with imported and costly cinnamon and nutmeg spices.

There is a sparkling and beautifully decorated community Christmas tree near Market Square, although the Christmas tree tradition was a German custom that arrived in America in the 1800s. Some sources say the custom was popularized as a result of an 1825 Philadelphia newspaper article. Purportedly, Charles Minnegrode, a German immigrant, brought the custom to Williamsburg in the 1840s. In those days, trees were decorated with strings of popcorn, dried fruits, cranberries, paper ropes, handmade paper ornaments, and candles that were lit for only a few minutes at a time. Trees were put up and decorated on Christmas Eve and removed at the end of the twelve days of Christmas.

Early settlers in America celebrated Christmas—considered a holy day (holiday) simply. In fact, the Puritans banned the holiday as pagan—and history traces many later customs to pagan origins—and Christmas wasn't legalized in Vermont until 1850. For the most part, Christmas was celebrated by early colonists by going to church (which was decorated with greens), fasting, and then feasting with family and friends. In those early days, homes were not decorated. The Victorians, who embraced the German customs, are credited with making home and family a more important part of the celebration of Christmas.

A Williamsburg Christmas, of course, is very special because it provides opportunities to witness and participate in festivities at church, historic houses, exciting shops and museum displays. For church, there's the venerable Bruton Parish Church on Duke of Gloucester Street, in the very heart of Historic Williamsburg. Some 80 historic houses have been preserved and restored. Many are open.

The quaint, beautifully decorated, and thoughtfully stocked shops make spending time and money a pleasurable, and occasionally even an educational experience. In shops such as the Silversmith shop, for example, it's possible to watch expert craftspeople create goblets, strainers, and other household objects in much the same way a colonial silversmith might have crafted these items.

There is also the DeWitt Wallace Decorative Arts Museum, with displays of furniture, prints, ceramics, metalwork and textiles… premier collection of folk art and numerous displays and exhibits.

There are musical entertainment galore. But perhaps its knowing that patriots to whom we owe so much once trod these beautiful streets that makes Christmas in Williamsburg entirely unique.

Colonial Williamsburg Foundation, a private, not-for-profit educational institution encourages experiencing Christmas in Williamsburg and the gifts, donations, and endowments that keep this America's living history town.

At the Ludwell-Paradise House, a plain ribbon-hung wreath enhances handsome windows featuring multi-panes. Deep reveals contain room-warming shutters with raised grounds, much copied in subsequent centuries. The window is dressed in a classic swag-and-jobot drapery designed by Colonial Williamsburg interior designers. *Photograph courtesy The Colonial Williamsburg Foundation.*

The Ludwell-Paradise House Dining Room with its traditional green-painted and paneled wall is decorated with greenery for the holidays. The long double-pedestal table, surrounded by Chippendale-style chairs, is set for a festive meal as it would have been when Williamsburg was the seat of Virginian culture. *Photograph courtesy The Colonial Williamsburg Foundation*

**Near Right:** Interpreter Bill Weldon plays a baroque guitar during a performance at Chowning's Tavern. *Photograph courtesy Colonial Williamsburg Foundation*
**Below and Far Right:** The handsome Williamsburg Inn is decorated in seasonal greenery, sparkling lights, and an eye-stopping Christmas tree for the Christmas holidays. *Photography courtesy The Colonial Williamsburg Foundation*

The joyous tree at The Williamsburg Inn. *Photograph courtesy of The Colonial Williamsburg Foundation.*

ENTRANCE ON SIDE

1. The door of the Peyton Randolph House is decorated with a cheerful pinecone-and-apple embellished evergreen swag and wreath as it would have been in the late 1770s. *Photograph courtesy The Colonial Williamsburg Foundation*

2. At the Prentis House, a wreath is enlivened with patriotically colored red, white and blue dried flowers. *Photograph courtesy The Colonial Williamsburg Foundation*

3. Inside the Margaret Hunter Shop, wreaths and seasonal ornaments hang from ribbons. *Photography courtesy The Colonial Williamsburg Foundation*

4. Interpreter Martha Millhouse, in period dress, pauses at the entrance of the Palmer House. *Photograph courtesy The Colonial Williamsburg Foundation*

1. Milliners Doris Warren and Brooke Wellborn re-enact the holiday season in Colonial Williamsburg. *Photographs courtesy The Colonial Williamsburg Foundation*

2. Interpreter Aislin Channon, in colorful period costume, holds a basket of mistletoe.

3. At the James Geddy Home, the young Geddy girls' custom of decorating the window with holly is reenacted during the Christmas holidays.

The Museums of Colonial Williamsburg's Folk Art Christmas tree. *Photograph courtesy The Colonial Williamsburg Foundation*

Gilded
Age
Grandeur

# 14.

## Whitehall

Palm Beach, Florida

### Christmas at Whitehall

"More wonderful than any palace in Europe, grander and more magnificent than any other private dwelling in the world," hailed the *New York Herald* when Henry Flagler unveiled Whitehall, his 55-room Beaux Arts estate in Palm Beach in 1902. Whitehall, designed by architects John Carrere and Thomas Hastings as a winter get-away for the railroad tycoon and his wife, is now a National Historic Landmark, open to the public as the Flagler Museum.

Throughout December, the Museum is decorated for Christmas in traditional Gilded Age splendor. Extensive research into turn-of-the-century holiday decorations by the Museum's staff makes Whitehall's holiday decoration historically accurate and unique. The decorations blend lush tropical plant materials such as magnolia, palm fronds, and Spanish moss with more traditional greenery, holly and poinsettias. Even the Christmas presents under the Grand Hall Tree have historically accurate wrappings.

The Annual Christmas Tree Lighting, held the first Sunday in December, is a tradition not to be missed. Throughout the afternoon, Christmas carols are played on Whitehall's 1249-pipe Odell organ. Carolers can be heard in the Museum's courtyard. The event culminates with the youngest descendants of Henry Flagler lighting the Christmas Tree in the Grand Hall. Those fortunate visitors who reserve a Holiday Evening Tour are treated to a special tour of Whitehall's Christmas decorations by the soft glow of its original light fixtures, carolers in the Museum's West Room, and holiday refreshments.

Diligent research effort and abundant materials in the Flagler archives offer visitors to Whitehall during the holidays a wonderful way to learn how many of today's holiday traditions began—late in the 19th century.

Perhaps even more interesting is to experience the beauty with which the Flagler's surrounded themselves and their friends.

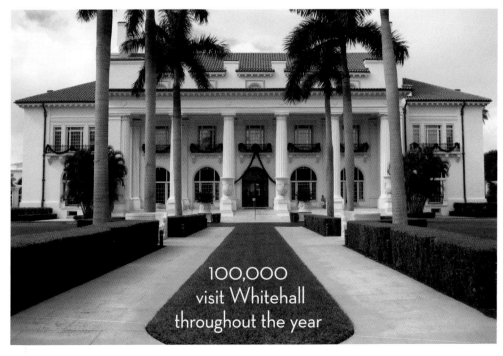

100,000 visit Whitehall throughout the year

**Near Left:** Whitehall, designed by Carrere and Hastings in a neoclassical style, boasts fifty-five rooms furnished in a variety of historic styles by the New York design firm of Pottier and Stymus. *Photograph courtesy Flagler Museum*
**Opposite:** Mary Lily Flagler and her female guests gathered in the Louis XVI-style Drawing Room, where there is a cameo of Marie Antoinette above each door and window. Aluminum leaf—as precious as gold during this era and coated with shellac for warmth—highlights plaster ornaments. *Photograph courtesy Flagler Museum*

Glorious

**Top:** The moment the youngest descendants of Henry Flagler light the tree in the annual evening ceremony, guests gasp as myriad colored bulbs begin their dance of dazzling light. Thousands visit during the holidays; 100,000 visit Whitehall throughout the year. *Photograph courtesy Flagler Museum. Photograph courtesy Flagler Museum*

**Above and Near Left:** Christmas and its music is celebrated in the Music Room, where, on the first Sunday in December—the day of the annual evening Christmas Tree Lighting ceremony— carols are played throughout the afternoon on Whitehall's 1249-pipe Odell organ. *Photograph courtesy Flagler Museum*

**Left:** Beneath a gloriously decorated ceiling (lowered at Henry Flagler's direction to create a sense of intimacy), the massive ceiling-high tree is the focal point of the 4,000 square foot Great Hall. *Photograph courtesy Flagler Museum*

A portrait of Henry Flagler's granddaughter, Jean Flagler Matthews, founder of the Henry Morrison Flagler Museum.
*Photograph courtesy Flagler Museum*

1249-pipe Odell organ

*Photograph courtesy Flagler Museum*

Draped garlands and vivid poinsettias decorate the magnificent twin staircases (called a double staircase) that lead from either side of a central landing in the Grand Hall. *Photograph courtesy Flagler Museum.*

1. Billiards was such a popular game that Flagler enlarged the room, altering original plans for the Billiards Room. The Caen stone mantel with Swiss-style decoration dominates the room with its decoratively painted ceiling and wall panels painted to resemble zebra oak. *Photograph courtesy Flagler Museum.*

2. Henry Flagler's portrait hangs above the fireplace in the Library, which is decorated in the masculine Italian Renaissance style. Wood-look ceiling beams with inset leather-look panels are actually molded and painted cast plaster and fabric—typical of craftsmanship and technology that made it possible to complete Whitehall in only eighteen months. *Photograph courtesy Flagler Museum*

3. Henry and his wife, Mary Lily Flagler, enjoyed breakfast at a set time daily in the Breakfast Room. Guests who were late ate in the nearby hotel! *Photograph courtesy Flagler Museum*

4. The Dining Room at Whitehall boasts an intricately painted ceiling decorated with rosettes with dolphin motifs, a custom rug that is recessed into the parquet floor, green silk walls, and a fireplace mantel carved with shells, crabs, and fruit. *Photograph courtesy Flagler Museum*

# 15.

## Tudor Place

Washington, D. C.

### Capitol Christmas

Tudor Place, in the nation's capitol, is a capital place to visit during the Christmas holidays. "At Christmas time this history-imbued house is decorated most beautifully. Today, decorations and events often center on a theme such as the Nutcracker, inspiration for 2006," says Heather A. Bartlow, director of communications and development.

"Tudor Place at Christmas time is alive with festive, memory-making activities for both adults and children. Among a number of educational and entertaining events is the popular annual workshop that teaches wreath-making to adults," Heather states. The notice for the Year 2008 event read: "Fashion your own holiday decorations using historic plant material from the Tudor Place Garden including cedar, magnolia leaves, berry-laden holly, pine cones and boxwood, with festive ribbon to add the finishing touch. Get a wonderful start on your holiday decorations." Using materials from Tudor Place sounds wonderful, but may not always be an option. If in doubt, ask.

According to Heather, "Another popular annual workshop teaches gingerbread making to children. And a children's ornament workshop teaches youngsters from ages 4-7 to create holiday ornaments using clay, papier-mache and acrylic paint."

Other workshops are introduced each holiday season. "Hits can become annual events, so look for repeats of the chocolate-making workshop introduced in 2008—it proved educational, entertaining, and in the best of taste!" Heather says.

Plans for the Christmas holidays, including themes, events, and a listing of workshops (which require both fees and reservations), are posted on the Tudor Place web site, a boon for visit planning.

**Above:** The south façade of Tudor Place in the summer features a unique domed entry; that is, one-half of the circular shape of the dome forms a demi-lune exterior portico, while the other half forms the convex exterior wall of the entry hall or "Saloon," as it was called. *Photograph courtesy Tudor Place*

**Right:** Tudor Place, built by Thomas Peter, the first mayor of Georgetown, for his wife Martha Custis, granddaughter of Martha Washington, overlooks the remaining 5-1/2 acres of the original 8-1/2 acres purchased in 1805. *Photograph courtesy Tudor Place*

THE
best of
taste

## Historic Background

*T*udor Place is tied to America's earliest history. In 1805, an 8-1/2 acre city lot, at 1644 31st Street NW, Washington, DC, was purchased by Thomas Peter, son of the first mayor of Georgetown, and his wife, Martha Custis, granddaughter of Martha Washington. The $8,000 purchase price was a legacy from George Washington.

Heather says, "The couple engaged Dr. William Thornton, a self-taught architect, to design their residence. The neo-classical style house, with its striking view of the Potomac River, is comprised of an impressive central structure flanked by wings. Buff-colored stucco covers the brick exterior. The façade is distinguished by a demilune temple-style entry porch. Completed in 1816, Tudor Place continued in the Custis-Peters family for 178 years."

**5.**

*Tudor Place*
Historic House & Garden
Washington, DC
1816

Image Adapted From Sketch by
Walter Gibson Peter
1894

**6.**

*Tudor Place*

**7.**

**8.**

1. The priceless clock under a protective glass dome that decorates the Drawing Room mantel is only one of the 8,000 items, including objects used by George and Martha Washington, that comprise the Tudor Place Collection. *Photograph by Heather Bartlow, courtesy Tudor Place*

2. The Kissing Ball, a tradition in America's early days, hangs at the entry to the Drawing Room. *Photograph by Heather Bartlow, courtesy Tudor Place*

3. Detail, The Kissing Ball. *Photograph by Heather Bartlow, courtesy Tudor Place*

4. The Staircase is treated to a swagged garland of seasonal greenery. *Photograph by Heather Bartlow, courtesy Tudor Place*

5 The contained Drawing Room is more formal than its Parlor counterpart directly across the entry hall (saloon), which opens into the Dining Room. A reception for the Marquis de Lafayette was held here in 1824. *Photograph courtesy Tudor Place*

6. A souvenir Christmas tree ornament bears an image of Tudor Place. *Photograph courtesy Tudor Place*

7. The popular annual wreath workshop at Tudor Place encourages hand-making wreaths using natural materials from the Tudor Place Gardens. *Photograph courtesy Tudor Place*

8. A Christmas Card features Tudor Place, a premier example of American neoclassical architecture, designed by Dr. William Thornton. *Photograph courtesy Tudor Place*

## Interior Highlights

"*T*he rooms of Tudor Place are architecturally and historically compelling," says Heather, noting these highlights:

The Saloon. A circular portico—called a saloon (from the French salon)—extends or continues into the interior the demilune shape of the entry, creating a "full-circle" effect and an outstanding architectural feature.

The Drawing Room, the more formal of two parlours, features cast plasterwork by Sam Collins, an African-American craftsman. Among historic events held in this room was an 1824 reception for the Marquis de Lafayette.

The less-formal Parlor has served as parlor, dining room and living room. Britannia Peter Kennon took in Union boarders during the Civil War. They ate in this room.

Dining Room. Martha Custis Peter and Mrs. William Thornton (wife of the architect) watched the burning of the U.S. Capitol by the British from the dining room window!

**Above and Opposite, top:** The Saloon (the British form of the French term for vestibule) delights with its uniquely shaped exterior wall overlooking the portico. The floor-to-ceiling glass seems to be curved, but actually only the woodwork curves. Center windows give access to the South lawn. *Photograph by Heather Bartlow, courtesy Tudor Place*

**Opposite, bottom:** Martha Custis Peter and Mrs. William Thornton (wife of the architect of both Tudor Place and the U.S. Capitol), watched the burning of the Capitol by the British from a window in this room which was then a bedroom. It became the Dining Room in the early 20th Century. *Photograph by Heather Bartlow, courtesy Tudor Place*

# The Collections

*S*ingle-family ownership of Tudor Place for 179 years marks it as a most remarkable repository of fascinating artifacts. "There are more than 8,000 items dating from 1750 to 1983, half of them on exhibit in the Main House," says Heather. Outstanding are:

*The Washington Collection* consists of over 100 objects that originally belonged to George and Martha Washington. Highlights include an outstanding 19th century American silver collection. Curators describe as "extraordinary" the Washington porcelain collection that includes a Sèvres dinner service and a Society of Cincinnati soup plate. There is also a Chinese Chippendale tea table and a unique waxwork by Samuel Fraunces of Fraunces Tavern in New York City. But, perhaps most exciting to historians and non-historians alike is the letter from George to Martha Washington—one of only three that exist!

A miniature of George Washington given to Martha Custis on the eve of her marriage to Thomas Peters is included in the large collection of fine jewelry from leading American jewelers. Among an extensive collection of paintings and drawings is a Thomas Cheeseman engraving of George Washington (after a painting by John Trumbull).

The Silver Collection includes a porringer dating to 1734 that was owned by Jacky Parke Custis, Martha Peter's father. There is a cake basket and serving pieces by Georgetown silversmith Charles Alexander Burnette, and pieces from Baltimore silversmith Samuel Kirk.

Other collections include sculpture, photographs, furniture. "Three-hundred linear feet of personal papers of the Custis-Peter family from the mid-18th century to 1984, comprise a rich trove of correspondence, diaries, financial records, inventories, blueprints, and architectural drawings," says Heather.

The gardens. The 5-1/2 acres of garden that remain, maintain much of the original Federal period. They also reflect changes made in the 19th and later centuries as Washington, DC grew up around Tudor Place. "At Christmas time, bare limbs and branches create natural sculpture worth noting from the warmth of welcoming rooms. But specimen trees, shrubs, and flowers will be better enjoyed when the winds of winter have disappeared," says Heather.

East and West meet in this Chinese export porcelain punch bowl with an interior scene of a Western foxhunt and an exterior rendering of Chinese rice cultivation—part of the Tudor Place ceramics collection from many countries and which spans over 200 years.
*Photograph by Heather Bartlow, courtesy Tudor Place*

The Tudor Place silver collection includes pieces by Georgetown silversmith Charles Alexander Burnett and a number in the Baltimore repousse style associated with Samuel Kirk of Baltimore. *Photograph by Heather Bartlow, courtesy Tudor Place*

Greek
Revival-style

# *16.*

## *Bartow-Pell Mansion*

Bronx, New York

### Come For Christmas On The Sound

Celebrating Christmas in the elegant Bartow-Pell Mansion Museum—an 1842 Greek Revival-style house situated on property purchased by Thomas Pell in 1654—is a rare privilege. The first of approximately twenty-two estates that at one time overlooked the Long Island Sound, the Bartow-Pell Mansion is the *only* residence to survive.

When the City of New York purchased the historic property in 1888 for the future Pelham Bay Park, the mansion was left unoccupied. In 1914, the newly-formed International Garden Club (now the Bartow-Pell Conservancy), headed by Mrs. Charles Hoffman, stepped in and raised funds to hire the distinguished Delano and Aldrich architectural firm to restore the house—nine years before Monticello was rescued! The

Bartow-Pell Conservancy, through the Bartow-Pell Landmark Fund, together with New York City's Historic House Trust and Department of Parks and Recreation, continues to maintain this historic site which celebrates Christmas in the Victorian style.

Plan to come at Christmastime to Bartow-Pell with its stunning views of the Long Island Sound *especially* for the candlelight tour. Docents and tour guides dressed in mid-19th-century period-style costumes tell of early Christmas traditions as they stroll through grand rooms furnished in the elegant neoclassical style, fancifully decorated for the holidays.

Christmas decorations each year are unique, but Amanda Kraemer, Education Assistant, describes the spirited 2008

**Opposite:** A ceiling-high Christmas tree in the Entry Hall, lavishly decorated with such interesting ornaments as a Snow Maiden, greets visitors during the holiday season. *Photograph by Tanya and Amanda Kraemer, courtesy Bartow-Pell Mansion Museum*

**Above:** The garden facade in winter. *Photograph by Tanya and Amanda Kraemer, courtesy Bartow-Pell Mansion Museum*

Christmas design: "Bartow-Pell was decorated with a Victorian-inspired interpretation of the Nutcracker Suite. Each room in the mansion featured a tree reminiscent of a dance or scene from that Ballet."

"The sweeping formal Double Parlors were decorated for a holiday dinner party. At each setting were Christmas crackers, invented by Tom Smith in 1847, when the Bartow family would have been celebrating one of the earliest Christmases in their new home.

"The more intimate Family Parlor was decorated for a private family Christmas. A table top tree—similar to the tree shown in a photograph of Queen Victoria and her family in 1841—was decorated with cranberry-and-popcorn strings, candy canes, pine bows, and candles.

"The Master Bedroom (with its famous Lannuier bed) featured Asian-inspired decorations. Fans, parasols and lanterns interpreted the Nutcracker's *Mandarin Tea Dance.*

"The Girls Bedchamber, using a blue-and-white colored winter scheme, recalled the *Snow Maiden's Dance.*"

Each Christmas, in addition to the candlelight tour of beautifully decorated rooms, magical music wafts throughout the house. At the end of the tour, mulled cider and tasty treats await.

**Above:** Early in the holiday season, wreaths on windows in the adjoining Solarium and a simple holiday floral arrangement in one of the Double Parlours hint of imminent full-blown holiday decorations soon to come. *Photograph by Tanya and Amanda Kraemer, courtesy Bartow-Pell Mansion Museum*
**Right:** Bartow-Pell Mansion, an outstanding neoclassical structure in the snow, is surrounded by magnificent garden. *Photograph by Tanya and Amanda Kraemer, courtesy Bartow-Pell Mansion Museum*

neoclassical
architecture

# A Brief History

$\mathcal{M}$ anor literature notes that this site predates colonial settlement. Here are key dates and events:

**1654,** Thomas Pell, an English physician from Connecticut, bought from the Siwanoy tribe vast acreage, including what is now the Bronx and lower Westchester.

**1666,** He received a royal patent to establish the Manor of Pelham.

**1677,** Sir John Pell, Thomas's nephew and heir build a Manor house. Inhabited by several generations, the house was destroyed during the American Revolution. Following the Revolution, John Bartow, husband of Ann Pell (daughter of the fourth Lord of the Manor), acquired the property.

**1813,** Hannah LeRoy, wife of Herman, a Dutch diplomat in New York City, bought the property. (Aaron Burr, a Bartow relative by marriage) witnessed this transaction.

**1836,** Robert Bartow, grandson of John, bought the property.

**1842,** The present mansion was built for Robert Bartow (who was in the paper and bookselling business in New York City and Norwich, Connecticut) and his wife, Maria Lorillard and their children.

**1888,** New York City bought the property for the future Pelham Bay Park.

**1914,** The International Garden Club was formed to save Bartow-Pell.

**1915,** Charles Whitman, Governor of New York, officially opened the house as the home of the Club.

**1926,** New York City Mayor Fiorello LaGuardia brought his staff to this Mansion on the Sound to escape the unusually hot City summer.

**1946,** Bartow-Pell opened as a museum.

**1977,** Bartow-Pell was designated a National Landmark

Colorful Oriental fans on the mantel join forces with other items to play up the Mandarin style decorations that carry out the Nutcracker theme chosen for Christmas at the Bartow-Pell Mansion. *Photograph by Tanya and Amanda Kraemer, courtesy Bartow-Pell Mansion Museum*

# Significant Furnishings

*T*he house is furnished in Neo-classical style furnishings by such noted makers as Duncan Phyfe, Joseph Meeks and Sons, and others. In addition to furnishings owned by the mansion, period pieces are on loan from the Metropolitan Museum of Art, Brooklyn Museum, Museum of the City of New York, and private collections.

Traditionally, there are two unusually noteworthy pieces on exhibit. A desk in the Upstairs Reception Area that belonged to Aaron Burr, who was married to Theodosia Bartow, will either be on display or at another site. The Lannuier Bed in the master bedroom (made by famed French cabinetmaker Charles Honorê Lannuier in 1825 for the Bell family of New York City) has the Lannuier label on the front rail. It is the only documented Lannuier bed with its original crown.

Lovers of historic houses and beautiful gardens will visit throughout the year; but, Christmas—when the gardens may be blanketed with snow, creating a winter wonderland—is a most special season at Bartow-Pell.

A desk said to have belonged to Aaron Burr, who was related to the Bartows by marriage, is shown displayed in the Family Parlor. *Photograph by Tanya and Amanda Kraemer, courtesy Bartow-Pell Mansion Museum*

**1.**

**2.**

**3.**

1. Appropriately costumed re-enacters greet arriving guests as Barbara Dennis does here, at the exciting Candlelight tour of the Bartow-Pell Mansion. *Photograph by Tanya and Amanda Kraemer, courtesy Bartow-Pell Mansion Museum*

2. In the Master Bedroom, the Lannier Bed with its ornate canopy (made for Mrs. Isaac Bell of New York City) is placed lengthwise along the wall in the the *lit à la française* style. Oriental fans on the Christmas tree help to temporarily transform the room into a Mandarin Tea Room, carrying out the Nutcracker theme. *Photograph by Tanya and Amanda Kraemer, courtesy Bartow-Pell Mansion Museum*

3. and Opposite: Candlelight casts an amber glow on the Formal Double Parlor (North and South, with fireplace) decorated for a Victorian Christmas. *Photograph by Tanya and Amanda Kraemer, courtesy Bartow-Pell Mansion Museum*

air of magic

# 17.

# Bingham-Waggoner Home and Estate

Independence, Missouri

## An Artists' Holiday House

Christmas begins early at the Bingham-Waggoner Estate—home of noted artist George Caleb Bingham, in Independence, Missouri, a town well known as home of the late American President, Harry S. Truman.

Tours of the impressive two-story house begin the day after Thanksgiving. On the first Sunday of December in the historic town of Independence, Missouri, there is a traditional Twilight Tour from 4 to 7 p.m. Townspeople say the lights twinkle just a little brighter and there is magic in the air. The tour features costumed guides at three historic sites: The Bingham-Waggoner Estate, Vaile Mansion and Marshall's House. At the Bingham-Waggoner Estate, a costumed Mrs.Santa tells stories to children and fresh baked cookies and spiced tea are sold in the modified tea room.

Beautiful holiday decorations welcome visitors to the classical Italianate style structure with its distinctive wrap-around porch. Inside, the house is richly furnished in the substantial style typical of the elegant Victorian era. About ninety-five percent of the furnishings are said to have belonged to original owners, which include three

**Near Left:** The Italianate 1879 house was home to artist and politician, George Caleb Bingham, painter of the famous "Order No. 11," a protest against the violence of governing Union troops. *Photographs by Janeen Aggen, courtesy Independence, Missouri Tourism*
**Below:** Bright Christmas greenery brings holiday cheer to the handsome entry. Photograph by Janeen Aggen, courtesy Independence, Missouri Tourism
**Opposite:** Trees throughout are lavishly adorned. *Photographs by Janeen Aggen, courtesy Independence, Missouri Tourism*

generations of the Waggoner family, who owned and occupied the house for almost one-hundred years. During that time, in the 1890s, the building was extensively renovated. Many of the furnishings date from this period.

The 1852 house (later known as the Bingham-Waggoner House) was built along the 1846 alignment of the Santa Fe Trail, then the highway for traffic flowing from the east to the riches-promising west. Noted artist George Caleb Bingham purchased the house and adjoining properties in 1864 and 1865. He soon deeded it to his second wife, Eliza, perhaps because of threats of Civil War and post-Civil war violence along this western border.

Bingham made his studio (no longer there) in a log-and-clapboard building to the northwest of his home. It was here that he painted his famous "Marshal Law" (known also as Order 11). Following a raid against Lawrence Kansas by William Quantrill and his band, General Thomas Ewing, Jr., commander of the District of the Border, ordered all persons living in Jackson, Cass, Bates and Vernon counties (except those living near large towns) to vacate their homes within fifteen days. Bingham protested by painting "Marshal Law," which depicted the ensuing chaos. He commissioned a large engraving which brought Bingham and his painting much publicity.

The politically active Bingham sold his home to Francis Eames in 1870. The Waggoner family, Pennsylvania millers, bought the house in 1879, and began operations in Independence. Bess Truman's material grandfather, George Porterfield Gates, became a partner and the company's "Queen of the Pantry Flour" became nationally known.

In 1979, the City of Independence purchased the home and its 19.5 acres, and made it a museum and park in tribute to travelers on the Santa Fe Trail—a living monument, never more alive than at Christmas time.

A profusion of toys, dolls, stockings, and decorations create a sense of delightful pandemonium—hallmark of the child-oriented Victorian Christmas. *Photographs by Janeen Aggen, courtesy Independence, Missouri Tourism*

Christmas trees throughout the the Bingham-Waggoner House, including the Library and Dining Room are thoroughly bedecked with a plethora of ornaments in the High Victorian style. *Photographs by Janeen Aggen, courtesy Independence, Missouri Tourism*

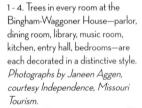

1 - 4. Trees in every room at the Bingham-Waggoner House—parlor, dining room, library, music room, kitchen, entry hall, bedrooms—are each decorated in a distinctive style. *Photographs by Janeen Aggen, courtesy Independence, Missouri Tourism.*

5. Bright Christmas greenery and big plaid bows bring holiday cheer to the handsome Entry Hall stairway with its polished paneled and carved wood walls and rich Turkey red oriental runner. *Photograph by Janeen Aggen, courtesy Independence, Missouri Tourism*

6. The buffet top in the Dining Room is swathed in greenery, ribbons, bright shiny and vividly colored ornaments and more...in the Victorian spirit of "more is better"—especially when it comes to decorating for Christmas. *Photographs by Janeen Aggen, courtesy Independence, Missouri Tourism*

7. In the Pink Parlor, warmly colored walls topped by a wide frieze with a delicate swag decoration create an elegant mood underscored by sumptuous Christmas decorations. *Photographs by Janeen Aggen, courtesy Independence, Missouri Tourism*

# *18.*

## *Vaile Mansion*

Independence, Missouri

### Vaile Mansion Magic

The Vaile Mansion is one of three houses in Independence, Missouri (home of the late President Harry S. Truman) included in a traditional 4 to 7 p.m. Twilight Tour that takes place on the first Sunday of December. Everyone agrees that all through the town lights sparkle and a magical mood prevails.

At all three houses—Vaile, Bingham-Waggoner and Marshall's—there are costumed guides. At Vaile, historic home of Harvey Merrick Vaile and his wife, Sophia, there is live music and visitors are treated to all the furbelows of the mature Victorian style. Decorations abound, with a profusion of ribbons, lace, cherubs, angels, garlands, bells, and exotic ornaments.

**Below:** Vaile, an outstanding 31-room mansion in the Second Empire or "General Grant style," in Independence, Missouri. *Photograph courtesy of Independence, Missouri Tourism*
**Right:** At the doorway which is decorated with garlands of greenery accented with red ribbon, a costumed maid greets holiday visitors. *Photograph by Janeen Aggen courtesy Independence, Missouri Tourism*

Curator Ron Potter says, "Every year at Christmas, the Vaile Mansion has a 'chandelier' tree which hangs upside down from the ceiling of the Grand Hall. This was a German tradition that Queen Victoria—who brought a tree into her castle and started the Christmas tree tradition—learned from her husband Prince Albert. It delights all visitors who enter the Mansion during the holidays."

The national newspaper, *USA Today,* described Vaile as a "Christmas Castle," and indeed, the holiday season is the climax of the year's focus on the 31-room mansion. The elegant Second Empire or French Renaissance style named for the reign of Napoleon III, is distinguished by several key features. Typically, the structure is three stories high, with an impressive central tower. Often, cupolas rise above the center of the roof, making the structure look even taller and more imposing. The most distinctive characteristic is the mansard roof—flat on top with convex or concave sides.

Called the first true style of the Victorian era, it was called the *General Grant* style because it was favored for administrative buildings during his administration. It was seen in the Northeast and Midwest, but infrequently elsewhere and seldom in domestic architecture. It is believed that the Vailes had seen the style in Normandy during a European trip.

Kansas City architect Asa Cross designed the building, which was completed in 1881, at a cost of $100,000. A Kansas City newspaper called it "the most princely, most comfortable house in the entire west." More recently, it is said to be the finest example of the Second Empire style in the United States.

The interior boasts elaborate architectural details, frescoes, and ornately painted ceilings. On the second floor of the mansion is a room called "Nature's Bower" which has hundreds of faces and creatures painted into the woodwork which peer out at visitors. According to Potter, "Tour guides point flashlights at some of the more amusing ones to show the artist's whimsical sense of humor." There is also fine woodwork and nine marble fireplaces.

Vaile owes its comfort to the latest technology, including gas (for light and heat), flushing toilets, and a 6,000 gallon

"the most princely, most comfortable house in the entire west."

built-in water tank. Princely amenities include a 48,000 gallon wine cellar, greenhouse and carriage house.

The house has received many special recognitions in recent years, including being placed on the National Register of Historic Places. It is an Independence Historic Landmark and winner of the Heritage Commission Distinguished Service Award.

The media, including television and national magazines and newspapers, find the Vaile Mansion intriguing and an ideal subject for editorials. Victorian Homes magazine and Country Victorian Christmas magazine have featured this house. National Geographic includes it in "Guide to America's Great Houses," and HGTV featured Vaile in "Christmas Across America."

Vaile made his money in real estate and as a U.S. Mail contractor and founder of the Star mail Routes. He was accused (falsely) of some misdeed in handling the mail and while in Washington for his defense, his wife died of an overdose of morphine. Following his acquittal, Vaile returned home. After his death in 1894, the house was used variously as a women's college, inn, private asylum and sanitarium, a mineral water company office, and a nursing home. Roger and Mary Dewitt acquired the house in 1960. When Mrs. Dewitt died in 1983, the house was given to the City of Independence.

The Vaile Victorian Society operates the Vaile Mansion which once again is a princely place and every December, a Christmas Castle.

**Right:** Tubs of evergreens flank the Entry. *Photograph courtesy Independence, Missouri Tourism*
**Below:** Vaile in the snow is picture-postcard pretty. *Photograph courtesy of Independence, Missouri Tourism*

A great deal of attention was given to the decorating of Victorian Christmas trees, which soon were carefully color-schemed and themed, making definite, memorable design statements from room-to-room and year-to-year. *Photograph courtesy Independence, Missouri Tourism*

1. The Hallway is ablaze with Christmas trees, wall and ceiling embellishments, and a table laden with decorations.

2. and 3. Color-schemed and themed trees reflect room decor.

4. and 5. Bold, fashionable colors for walls at Vaile, which inspire similar color schemes in today's interiors, are a vivid backdrop for holiday decorations throughout the mansion.

6. A tree at the entry greets guests.

7. No room was ignored or left undecorated. Even the Kitchen was decorated, inspiring cooks who created the lavish meals and treats associated with the year's greatest holiday.

8. A dramatic large-scale urn filled with dried flowers and plants echoes the rich color scheme of Sitting Room and Music Room walls.

9. and 10. No surface—mantel, tabletop, piano, bookcase, shelf, dresser, or other—is left undecorated in a Victorian home, especially at Christmas. The more well-to-do the owners, the more and the fancier are decorations. 11. and 12. A great deal of attention is given to decorating trees in the bedrooms, especially when red and green just won't do. 13. Vaile Mansion's brilliant red walls—daring in their day and very much in style in the 21st century—make it easy to get into the spirit of a holiday tea served by a costumed maid. *Photographs courtesy Independence, Missouri Tourism*

# 19.

## David Davis Mansion

### Elegant Clover Lawn at Christmas

Boughs of evergreens fill the house with fragrance. Simulated gaslight bathes the rooms in a soft glow. The 36-room David Davis Mansion in Bloomington, Illinois at Christmastime becomes a sensory delight, a vision of Victorian elegance. It is always decorated for the season in the late-Victorian style, popular when this house was occupied by George P. Davis, son of Judge David and Mrs. Sarah Davis, who built the beautiful home known as Clover Lawn, in the 1870s.

In the sitting room, a stunning 12-foot tree is aglitter with exquisite ornaments true to those of the era that turned ornament-making into an art form, to the delight of generations of passionate collectors. These included glass figurative ornaments (many decorated with crinkled silver wire), cotton-batting figures decorated with crepe paper and tinsel, hand-blown heavy glass globes called kugels, and Dresdens, which Dr. Marcia Young, Director, describes as "the most exquisite paper ornaments ever made." Authentic decorations from 1870 to 1910 (the golden era of ornament making, says Dr. Young), are exhibited at the David Davis Mansion. Among the items on display are Raphael Tuck paper toys, crepe paper and scrap paper dolls, lead-weighted candle holders, wax angels, beaded tin decorations, and electric light bulbs in the shape of Santas, fruits, and flowers.

Dr. Young describes the parlor: "This cozy room served as a refuge and a sanctuary, protecting the Davis family from what Victorians feared was the corrupt world of the marketplace. The fireplace in this room was one of two in the mansion that were altered to burn wood. Apparently all eight of the home's fireplaces originally had coal grates with closed fronts. Writers, such as Catharine Beecher, lamented the 'modernity' of such devices; they robbed people of the pleasure of a bright, crackling, open fire. Sarah's wood-burning fireplaces proved to be a godsend in late 1872, when an epidemic among the horses in Bloomington meant that there were no coal deliveries for quite some time."

"Throughout the house—from parlor to pantry—are fifteen or more trees, each imaginatively decorated," says Dr. Young. "There may be a traditional Pennsylvania Dutch snow tree, five German goose feather trees, and trees hung with glass figural ornaments, cotton-batting figures, hand-blown glass globes (called kugels), Dresdens (exquisite paper ornaments), Raphael Tuck paper toys, crepe paper and scrap paper dolls, lead-weighted candle holders, wax angels, and beaded tin decorations—some rare, all captivating."

Dr. Young says that a truly special tree is the "upside-down" tree—a tree suspended top-side-down from the thirteen-foot high ceiling—an old European custom.

**Left:** Serene by day, after sundown during the Christmas holidays, the 36-room David Davis Mansion (in the Italianate Second Empire style popular during the mid-Victorian era) comes vividly alive with the enchanting lights and sounds of an Edwardian Christmas. *Photograph by Patricia Schley, courtesy David Davis Mansion*
**Opposite:** Mrs. Davis named her favorite room the Pink Chintz Room. It features a portrait of Judge Davis by the famous artist, G.P.A. Healy of Washington, D.C. *Photograph by Ken Kashian, courtesy David Davis Mansion*

1.

2.

Each Christmas tree at the David Davis Mansion, in the Victorian tradition, has a very special ornament—a glass pickle—hidden among its branches. Dr. Young assures that, "Good luck during the coming year is promised to the fortunate finder of the lucky glass pickle!"

A very special tree during Christmas 2006 was a unique tree—one featured in December 2005 at a special exhibit (Christmas at the White House) at the Abraham Lincoln Presidential Museum in Springfield, Illinois. According to Dr. Young, the connection between the elder Davis (a lawyer, U.S. Supreme Court Justice, U.S. Senator from Illinois, and businessman) and Abraham Lincoln is one of a long and lasting friendship. "That friendship began soon after they met in December 1835 and continued for thirty years. Davis helped Lincoln win the nomination as the Republican Party's presidential candidate in 1860, and served as Lincoln's appointee to the U.S. Supreme Court. Over the years, Judge Davis and his family amassed 19,000 letters, photos, and other items that were donated to what is now known as the Abraham Lincoln Presidential Library in Springfield, Illinois," she says.

When David Davis was appointed to the U.S. Supreme Court in 1862, his wife Sarah had no desire to live in Washington. "Judge Davis commissioned French-born architect Alfred Piquenard, a leading Midwestern architects whose commissions included the state capitol buildings in Springfield, Illinois and Des Moines, Iowa, to design the three-story structure that combines Italianate and Second Empire features found in mid-Victorian-style houses. It was built at Davis's farm, known as Clover Lawn, which was one of the many real estate investments that made him the largest landowner in Illinois (an estate valued at his death at more than four million dollars)," Dr. Young notes.

The house was constructed of yellow brick, with indoor plumbing for hot and cold water, gas lighting, a coal-fired furnace, and coal-burning fireplaces. Sarah later converted the sitting room fireplace to burn wood—"a godsend at a time in 1872 when no coal deliveries were made because of an epidemic among the horses," Dr. Young states.

The home was fitted with rare Italian marble, luxurious English carpeting, and fine French glass. Richly furnished interiors welcomed family and friends over the years, who worked together to form a society that transformed America's raw and rough western frontiers into orderly and prosperous communities, creating a unique nation among nations.

The house was donated in 1960 to the State of Illinois. It was entered in 1975 on the National Register of Historic Places. Dr. Young says, "Today, the public is welcomed to the David Davis Mansion, a National Historic Landmark and a world of Christmas splendor, where a taste of Christmas includes marzipan, sugarplums, mincemeat pies, plum pudding and a uniquely Victorian delight—chocolate cockroaches. The Victorians loved candies shaped like animals and insects and the chocolate cockroach was a favorite!" The David Davis Mansion State Historic Site is administered by the Illinois Historic Preservation Agency. The David Davis Mansion Foundation and the Agency are co-sponsors of *Christmas at the David Davis Mansion.*

1. In the sitting room, refuge and sanctuary for the politically and socially active Davis family, a putz or village (popularized by Germans in the early 20th Century, springs up at the base of a tall Christmas tree, decorated with a rare collection of circa 1870-1910 ornaments. The French-made brass and marble clock on the mantel, a housewarming gift, features sculptures of an Indian in a canoe and two mermen—typical of the Victorian love of the exotic.

2. The tree in the Pink Chintz Room is decorated with antique "scrap" paper ornaments.

3. Elaborate window treatments create a stage-like backdrop for a bedroom Christmas Tree.

4. High Victorian style interiors typically included large-scale floral carpets, elaborate window treatments, and heavily carved and embellished mahogany furniture like these.

5, 6, 7. The extensive and notable David Davis collection of antique dolls and toys—which includes a teddy bear tea party—serve as decorations in several bedrooms during Christmas.

8. Pots of poinsettias brighten the library of Yale-educated Judge Davis.

9. Most of the Mansion's wood-burning fireplaces were replaced by coal stoves like the one in this bedroom. The tabletop tree is covered in faux snow made of cotton batting, a popular decoration.

10. In the gracious dining room, Mrs. Sarah Davis presided over countless teas and dinners. Photographs by Ken Kashian, courtesy David Davis Mansion

3.

# 20.

## Emlen Physick Estate

Cape May, New Jersey

### Cape May in December

*Welcome, everything.*
*Welcome, alike what has been,*
*and what never was,*
*and what we hope may be,*
*to your shelter*
*underneath the holly,*
*to your places round the Christmas fire,*
*where what is sits open-hearthed!*

—Charles Dickens

**Above:** The "stick style" Dr. Emlen Physick Estate home is a landmark in Cape May, an authentic historic Victorian-style town on the New Jersey Shore and an all-seasons resort. Gardens of the Physick House, originally supplied by a greenhouse on the estate which also furnished winter greenery, welcome visitors in spring and summer to the quaint Victorian-looking seaside town. *All photography courtesy of Mid-Atlantic Center for the Arts.*

**Opposite:** Candles added excitement to the Physick's Christmas tree, which would have been decorated thematically—perhaps with patriotic mini-American flags. Servants who lit the candles just before the family and their friends entered the room, stood by with a bucket of water! They doused candle flames immediately following the departure of the diners.

Charming Cape May, the Victorian seaside resort located at the southernmost tip of New Jersey, along the beautiful southern shore, is more than merely a summer resort. It observes the Christmas season with a series of events. At the center of the town's 19th-century style celebration is the Emlen Physick Estate, Cape May's only Victorian house museum.

The Emlen Physick Estate, built in 1879, stands out among the town's other Gingerbread style homes by virtue of its Stick Style architecture. Stick Style is characterized by a grid work of raised boards (stickwork) overlaying clapboarded walls to create geometric decorative elements, according to Mid-Atlantic Center for the Arts (MAC), which operates the Physick Estate and the 1859 Cape May Lighthouse. The stickwork (or half-timbering), brackets, rafters, and braces are purely decorative elements that imitate medieval architecture. (Stick Style houses differ from later Tudor Revival houses sided with stucco, stone, or brick because of their wood construction.)

At the time, the Cape May Ocean Wave reported "the erection of a handsome villa, after a design different from any yet introduced at Cape May" that "when completed will doubtless be one of the very handsomest on the island" (June 22, August 29, 1878). The Physick house's news-making architecture was indeed very different from the other more conservative Italianate, Gothic and Mansard styles in Cape May.

Physick House's irregular, asymmetrical forms and roof lines, boxy projections—its bays, wings and towers—gave the building "character," a term used by Victorian architecture

character
and personality

**Top:** Servants hung live evergreen garlands from the dining room's gas-fueled "gasolier" chandelier, which they hastily lit just before family and guests entered the room, and quickly turned off when diners finished the ten-course dinner.
**Above:** In the hallway with its rich wood paneling in the Victorian style, seasonal garlands decorate doorways in the same way the Physicks would have decorated.

critics to suggest a house's "personality." The strong vertical emphasis —tall windows, multiple stories, surface ornamentation—give this Stick Style house an angular appearance that contrasts with the more curvaceous appearance of Gingerbread houses.

The Physick House, built by the bachelor doctor Emlen Physick for his extended family, is attributed to architect Frank Furness who is now recognized as one of this country's greatest Victorian architects. He designed more than 600 buildings in the greater Philadelphia area during the late-19th and early-20th centuries. His work fell out of favor and many of his buildings, including his office, were razed. Indeed, the under-appreciated architectural style did not have a name until almost 100 years later.

Historians believe that Furness is the only architect who could have designed the Physick House despite the lack of documentation. Historians point to the trademark features as the greatly oversized corbelled (upside down) chimneys, jerkinhead dormers, and porch brackets that appear in many other Furness buildings of the period, according to MAC. (For more on styles of the era, see Vincent Scully's *The Stick Style and the Shingle Style*.)

Dr. Physick died in 1916 and the estate passed through many hands, fell into disrepair, and was finally sold to developers who wanted to tear the house down to make room for tract housing. To save this vital piece of Cape May history, concerned citizens formed the Mid-Atlantic Center for the Arts (MAC) in 1970 and in 1973 (through the efforts of MAC) the City acquired the estate and leased it to MAC. MAC has restored the property, largely with money raised from MAC-initiated tours.

During the season which starts around the third week on November and runs through the first of January, the entire town of Cape May celebrates their Victorian heritage. The town spares nothing in recreating the sights and sounds, the tastes and aromas of 19th century festivities., so that Victorian inns, decked in their unique holiday finery, offer the hospitality of a bygone era, according to Jean Barraclough, Director of Marketing and Communications for MAC.

The Carriage House at the Physick Estate becomes a true "Christmas fantasyland" with recreations of holidays of years past with antique and vintage Santas and model trains, trees and toys. The annual Dickens Christmas Extravaganza offers a chance to experience a treasured work of the master storyteller. At the Gala Dickensian Feast, people come dressed as their favorite Dickens' character or in Victorian dress for a four-course Victorian Feast. (In the Physick's day, the meal would have been ten courses, lasting well into the evening, according to Robert E. Heinly, Ed.D., Museum Education Coordinator of the Mid-Atlantic Center for the Arts (MAC).

Inside the Physick house rooms are decorated as they would have been when Dr. Physick was at home there. "Decorations would have been done by the servants under the direction of Dr. Physick's mother, Mrs. Frances Ralston," says Dr. Heinly. "Unusual touches (to moderns) would be the use of poinsettias grown in the estate's greenhouse as cut flowers, and the hanging of live evergreen garland over the gasoliers [gas-burning lighting fixtures]. The tree, the center of the celebration, would have been illuminated by live candles." He points out that the tree candles and gasoliers were only lit by a servant just before the family and guests entered the room. "That same servant," says Dr. Heinly, "would keep a bucket of water and sponge on a stick always at the ready and would use same to douse the candles when the family and friends left the room. The gasolier would be turned off at this time also."

Then the Christmas tree would have been decorated with such edibles as cookies, nuts, fruits and strings of popcorn, which visiting children would eat. (Don't expect that to happen now!) Today's tree is more likely

decorated with a theme popular during that time period when miniature American flags were in vogue.

Dr. Heinly says that since the Physicks were the town's leading family, "Carolers would have visited early in the evening and been invited indoors for some wassail and cookies."

Nowadays, visitors to Cape May are treated to special "tours." The town's extensive offerings: *A Taste of Christmas, Candlelight House, Lamplighter House, Cape May Interiors,* and *Tea Tours.* Special "Ride" events include: *Evening Holly Trolley, Evening Wassail, Santa Trolley,* and *Ghosts of Christmas Past Trolley Rides.* The Holiday Crafts Fair offers arts and crafts. Two Equity theater companies, Cape May Stage and the East Lynne Theatre Company, produce popular holiday shows. Special workshops and seminars are offered including the *Holiday Traditions Workshop and Lunch* and lectures about Victorian life. For gourmets and wine lovers, there is the *Mad Batter Wine Tasting Dinner, Holiday Cooking School and Lunch, Cape May Wine School,* and *Holiday Chefs' Dine-Around.* A visit to Cape May and the Emlen Physick Estate at Christmastime is the perfect antidote for even the most jaded Christmas spirit," according to Jean Barraclough. "It's truly a step back in time to an old-fashioned era of holiday spirit."

In Dr. Physick's day, servants draped homegrown live evergreen garlands across heavily carved oak mantels and around windows and doorways.

# 21.

## *Pittock Mansion*

Portland, Oregon

### Oregon's Christmas Trail

Christmas at Pittock Mansion is one of Portland, Oregon's most popular and cherished holiday pilgrimages. During the holiday season, the house with its glowing lights, vivid poinsettias, velvet ribbons and wreaths, antique toy wooden horses, model trains and dolls evokes visions of joyous daily life and happy holidays during the Roaring '20s.

The mansion was home to pioneers Henry and Georgiana Pittock, from 1914 to 1919. The couple—he was in his eighties, she in her sixties—commissioned architect Edward Foulkes to design the residence in 1909. By 1914, the building was complete. The eclectic design incorporated English, French and Turkish, elements, along with a central vacuum system, intercoms, and indirect lighting.

The Pittocks utilized materials from the Northwest and employed Oregon craftsmen and artisans to build the house. The estate encompasses not only the mansion but also and Italianate gate lodge servants' quarters, garage, a greenhouse, gardens and grounds. "A house of historical significance and visual magnificence, the Pittock Mansion today offers us a uniquely personal opportunity to peek into the past, and study our world as it was, from the perspective of one family," say Pittock's historians.

Henry Lewis Pittock, born in England, traveled to Oregon on a wagon train from Pennsylvania in 1853 at the young age of 19, according to Pittock Mansion's preservationists. He was, and in his own words, "barefoot and penniless" when he arrived in Portland. He took a position at Thomas Jefferson Dryer's Weekly Oregonian newspaper. Less than seven years later, Pittock took ownership of newspaper in 1860 and changed its format to the daily paper—*The Oregonian*—that it is today. A consummate businessman, he built an empire that included banks, railroads, real estate, steamboats, sheep ranching, silver mining, and pulp and paper industry.

Historians say that the same year that he acquired the paper, the 26 year-old Pittock married Georgiana Martin Burton, a 15-year-old Missourian who had traveled across the plains from Keokuk, Iowa to Oregon Territory six years earlier. The couple's "long life of work, community service, and devotion to family ... would last 58 years and celebrate six children and eighteen grandchildren," according to the Mansion's historians.

The couple "was known for their quiet reserve, helpful demeanor, and love for the outdoors." Georgiana held an avid interest in gardening. Her terraced garden at the Mansion was known for its wide-breadth of blooms. She is also recognized for establishing the annual Rose Festival. Henry, an outdoorsman, rode horses in the Rose Festival parades and was among the first party to climb Mt. Hood. As legend has it, when another member of the climbing party suggested that the group sit down for a rest, Henry responded philosophically, "The man who sits down never reaches the top."

The couple lived in the mansion until their deaths—she in 1918 at the age of 72, and he in 1919 at 84. The mansion remained in the family's possession until 1958. Concerned citizens, alarmed by the threat of demolition and storm damage, raised funds to preserve the site in the early Sixties. Recognizing the estate's history, the City of Portland purchased it for $225,000 and opened to the mansion to the public in 1965.

**Below:** The Pittock Mansion, which sets 1,000 feet above the city of Portland commanding breathtaking views of the Cascade Mountains, is itself a beautiful scene in winter and summer. Its "Old World," mainly French Renaissance style, combines elements of French, several English, and Turkish architectural styles. It's impressive scale and exterior of Tenino stone from Tenino, Washington make the Mansion both imposing and intriguing. *Photograph by Michael Henley, Contemporary Images*
**Opposite:** Pots of scarlet poinsettias are emphatic accents for the elegant staircase made of Italian Tournelle buff marble. The handrail is of American southern gumwood. *Photograph by Bill Enos*

**1.**

**4.**

**2.**

**5.**

**6.**

**3.**

**7.**

**8.**

1–6. Bedrooms throughout the Mansion are chock full of Christmas decorations sure to appeal to children. These include loads of dolls, stuffed animals (including rabbits on a White Rabbit Tree and stuffed bears to play up the theme of "A Teddy Bear Christmas at the Pittock Mansion"), a faux Santa, and toys galore (including tiny red-sled ornaments on one garland).

7 and 8. The Dining Room overlooks the beautiful Pittock Mansion gardens. Garlands decorate the wide windows without obstructing views.

9. The bright, cheerful Music Room, beautifully decorated by The Northwest Society of Interior Designers, is a hit with thousands of visitors who make the Pittock Mansion an annual holiday destination.

10 and 11. Gaily wrapped Christmas presents and a tree decorated with sparkling lights and ornaments enliven the cozy Library with its Philippine mahogany paneling and elaborate bargework ceiling.

*Photographs by Bill Enos, courtesy Pittock Mansion*

**9.**

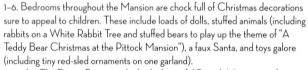

**10.**

**11.**

The unique Turkish Smoking Room features a beautiful small dome intricately decorated in a Moorish pattern. The Christmas tree adds a seasonal note.
*Photograph by Michael Henley, Contemporary Images*

larger-than-life

# 22.

## Molly Brown House

### Colorado Christmas

Most of America's historic houses are monuments to successful men; but while a self-taught mining engineer's fortune purchased the house at 1340 Pennsylvania Street, a woman made it famous. National fame came to Molly Brown after she survived the *Titanic* disaster and entered powerful national social circles

In 1886—a time when women were self-effacing homebodies, while men sought adventure and economic opportunity—Margaret (Molly) Tobin Brown (1867-1932) moved to Leadville, a Colorado mining town, in search of adventure and wealth. She found both when she met and married J. J. Brown, who soon discovered one of the largest veins of gold ever found in Colorado. Suddenly millionaires, the couple moved to Denver, purchased an impressive house, and entered Denver society.

> …this Christmas, perhaps, is the happiest, because it is the one most fresh in my memory, and we always think the joy of the moment greater than that of the past," Molly Brown wrote in the December 22, 1900, issue of the *Denver Post*.

Noting that Molly and J. J. celebrated Christmas 1900, with their two children and Molly's brother's family (which included three young nieces), museum literature relates:

> Denver would have been a fun place for this large family to celebrate. The poles along 16th Street near the Brown's home were decorated with wreaths and ice-skating was permitted on the City Park Lake. The Lyceum Theater presented a special Christmas Operetta for Children, and the *Denver Post* sponsored a Children's Carnival and Street

Fair where a brass band provided music and each child was given a bag of candy, an orange, and an apple. Margaret (Molly) was very involved in charitable functions and helped sponsor a Christmas Dinner and Toy Fair for local underprivileged children, held at the Brown Palace Hotel. She and J.J. also sent Christmas gifts and supplies to the families of miners in Leadville, where they had made their fortune in 1893.

The Browns decorated their house with true Victorian more-is-never-too-much style. One Christmas tree graced the Library. On the second floor another tree was decorated especially for their two children. Strings of electric lights cost twelve dollars a strand, but the Brown's could afford lots of lights, and their up-to-date house was wired for electricity.

Capitol Hill in 1880s Denver, was an elite enclave, home of the lucky few like Isaac and Mary Large, who had made a fortune in silver mining. They paid $4,000 for the land and in 1886, commissioned architect William Lang, whose design for their home deftly combined elements of Queen Anne, Richardson Romanesque, and neo-Classicism. Equally eclectic materials included rugged rhyolite to contrast with smooth red sandstone, stained glass windows, ornamental wood panels, and ornamental trim. The result was an exterior that was both dignified and romantic. Interiors were treated with the same skilful balance of exuberance and restraint. When the Larges fortune declined, they sold their home in April, 1894, to the Browns for $30,000.

Title to the house on Capitol Hill went to Margaret Tobin Brown in 1898. In the years that she lived in the house, she was incredibly active in social issues of the day, struggling against such giants of American industry as J. D. Rockefeller over the rights of coal miners. She supported suffrage leaders, and was passionate about art and drama.

Kerri Atter, Director/Curator of the house says, "Margaret Brown was a woman who lived ahead of her times. As we follow her life we become aware of the dramatic changes that shaped American history. Margaret had a unique ability to have

**Opposite:** The exterior of the Molly Brown House reveals an eclectic mix of Queen Anne, Richardson Romanesque, and neoclassical architectural elements. *Photograph by Jeff Padrick, King Studios; courtesy Molly Brown Museum.*

her finger on the pulse of change. She ran for Senate three times—*before woman had the right to vote nationally.* Here in Denver she was involved in much of the civic development that occurred at the turn of the century. For example she contributed one-fourth of the total finances to establish the Denver Dumb Friends league. She was Denver's first preservationist—saving the home of Poet Eugene Field. She was also a world traveler visiting exotic countries such as Japan, India, South Africa, Egypt, Cuba and South America."

Molly Brown was unsinkable, intrepid, and a star in an era of larger-than-life personalities, most of them men. In the years before her death in 1932, Molly Brown (separated from J.J.), lived elsewhere and rented out her house which fell into great decline. Through the efforts of Art Leisenring (who had purchased the house in 1958), and Ann Love, the Governor's wife, a group of concerned citizens organized themselves as Historic Denver, Inc. and bought the house for $80,000 on December 11, 1970. With the help of supporters, they began restoring the Unsinkable Molly Brown's house to its original Victorian splendor.

Beginning with the "'Twas the Night Before Christmas Candlelight Tour & Reading," each Christmas at The Molly Brown House is, perhaps, the best!

1. Not every room is decorated "to the teeth" for Christmas at the Molly Brown House, when all that's needed is a scarlet red table cloth on a table set with crystal decanters. 2. The Dining Room boasts a superbly decorated ceiling. The table is set for a formal dinner, with tall white tapers adding a sophisticated *avant garde* singular holiday note. 3. Flamboyant red walls and a mantel full of red-and-white striped stockings strike a high holiday note in the home of Denver's Unsinkable Molly Brown.

**Opposite:** In the Parlor, a Victrola and upright piano are ready for sing-along caroling near the gaily decorated Christmas tree. *Photographs by Jeff Padrick, King Studios; courtesy Molly Brown Museum*

# 23.

## *Bidwell House*

Monterey, Massachusetts

### Magic in Monterey

"What is perhaps most magical about the Bidwell House is its incredible setting," says Joseph P. Gromacki, Board Member, American Heritage Society.[1] "Surrounding the house are extensive stone outcroppings and terraced stone walls brimming with perennial beds and historic Colonial gardens." Each year in season, volunteer Garden Angels prepare the heirloom vegetable and flower gardens and the community gathers for an Early Winter festivity that is prelude to Christmas—the most magical time of the year.

Who could say nay to visiting Bidwell House, an authentic circa 1750 saltbox, at any time of the year? Wendell Garrett, Vice President of Decorative Arts, Sotheby's New York describes it as, "A gem. The most perfect example of a New England country home in its feeling, appearance and continuing daily life." [2]

**Below:** The Manse, built for Adonijah Bidwell in 1750 in Monterey, near Great Barrington, Massachusetts. *Photograph by Paul Rocheleau, courtesy The Bidwell House Museum*
**Right:** The Entry Door with its handsome overlight wears a Christmas wreath. *Photograph by Paul Rocheleau, courtesy The Bidwell House Museum*
**Opposite:** An adjustable candle stand in the Entryway is ready to light the way up the stairs. Beyond is a glimpse of the dining room. *Photograph by Paul Rocheleau, courtesy The Bidwell House Museum*

On a starry night, candles will light your way past the Iron Kettle bonfire to the original 1750 front door with blacksmith-made hinges and latches. Music, food, drink and the spirit of your neighbors will greet you as you enter the "Magical Monterey Moment." Gather around the fireplaces in an authentic New England party at Bidwell House.

*Who could resist such an invitation?*

JOYOUS
atmosphere

"Three generations of Bidwells inhabited this home," says Martha L. Dailey, PhD, Executive Director of The Bidwell House Museum. Changes were made over the years, but in 1960, Jack Hargis and David Brush purchased the house and began an extensive twenty-five year effort to restore and recreate the home of the Reverend Bidwell, guided by his 1784 inventory. At their bequests, The Bidwell House Museum was formed in 1990. Extensive collections and programs make it a must visit site for all.

Looking back. The Manse, as Bidwell House was called, was built in 1750 for Adonijah Bidwell, a Yale graduate and the first minister in Monterey, near Great Barrington. Today, Monterey is in the heart of the famed Berkshires, a favorite summer resort area and a cultural haven. But in 1754, Monterey was a waystop for travelers from Boston to Albany, New York enroute to the meeting of representatives from the thirteen colonies called by Benjamin Franklin. Dr. Dailey says, "Then, the Old Boston to Albany Post Road passed by the stately Georgian classic saltbox. Reverend Bidwell had stepped across the threshold of the front door with his new bride, Theodosia Colton, just two years before. The imposing house has the very same front door with original hardware made by a local blacksmith. Four fireplaces rise up from the center of a stone-arched foundation. These rooms have retained their original paneling in red oxide or verdigris and make a perfect setting for a Christmas celebration."

Dr. Dailey points out, of course, that early Puritans did not celebrate Christmas. But, "Christmas décor by the 1850s would be reminiscent of a Currier and Ives print. A balsam wreath with home made decorations or winter berries graced the doors and the hearth. As for decorum, the strict rules of the earlier Covenanted Congregationalists relaxed and singing with shape-note manuals was introduced." She notes that the bonfire that greets guests these days is a new use for a giant potash kettle "used by the earliest inhabitants to produce income in an economy of self-sufficiency." The house now, as it was then, is simply decorated for the holidays with greenery.

Describing life at The Manse in the early years, Dr. Dailey says, "If bedrooms were occupied, guests appreciated a space on the floor of the spacious Keeping Room. They slept with their feet to the fire. Mrs. Bidwell kept the home fires burning with tinder lit by a spark from the friction created by striking flint against steel."

Being hostess of The Manse was hard work. "She had two bee hive ovens that were almost always in operation. Good works translated to good food for needy members of the congregation," says Dr. Dailey. And, although these Puritans did not observe Christmas, there were plenty of other celebrations, including Election Day ceremonies, Barn Raisings, and Corn Husking parties. So many that the Reverend Bidwell had five punch bowls in his estate inventory at his death in 1784. Dr. Dailey says, "Enough hard cider was processed and kept in cellar barrels to keep a joyous atmosphere through the long New England winter." And perhaps a very merry Christmas season.

## Notes

1. The Scrivener, Milwaukee Art Museum, Fall/Winter 2006, "The Reverend Bidwell House," Joseph P. Gromacki, Board Member, American Heritage Society.

2. Ibid.

1. Sarah Wing in a Period costume is part of a family with fifth-generation roots in the Monterey area. *Photograph by Paul Rocheleau, courtesy The Bidwell House Museum*

2. The "two hearts door" leads from the Entrance Hall to the Living Room. The reason for the two hearts design remains a mystery. *Photograph by Paul Rocheleau, courtesy The Bidwell House Museum*

3. Dining Room furniture is American-made, dating from the mid- to late 1700s. At the table are Hudson River Valley sidechairs. The corner cupboard is original to the house. *Photograph by Paul Rocheleau, courtesy The Bidwell House Museum*

4. The Best Chamber (second floor east bedroom) bed coverlet dates from the late 18th century. Bed hanging are recent Indian crewelwork. *Photograph by Paul Rocheleau, courtesy The Bidwell House Museum*

5. The Best Parlor Chamber (second floor west bedroom) features a bed from the early 1800s. The coverlet is a quilt from Bidwell's extensive antique quilt collection. *Photograph by Paul Rocheleau, courtesy The Bidwell House Museum*

6. and 7. American redware at Bidwell includes pieces made by renowned New England potteries in Gonic, New Hampshire; Goshen, Connecticut; and Norwalk, Connecticut. Potters represented include Brooks Brothers, John Howard Corliss, and John M. Safford. *Photograph by Paul Rocheleau, courtesy The Bidwell House Museum*

1. The Best Parlor is decorated with wreaths during the holidays. *Photograph by Paul Rocheleau, courtesy The Bidwell House Museum*

2. and 3. The Bidwell intricate 17th century "casket" is a small box for valuables. It is covered in embroidered linen that is applied to panels and assembled on a wooden base by a cabinetmaker who supplied silver hinges, feet and locks. *Photograph by Joanne Jennings, courtesy The Bidwell House Museum*

4. Bidwell's veilleuse (pronounced vay-euz) is a food warmer of glazed earthenware made by Lambeth delft (1750-`1755). It consists of a cylindrical hollow pedestal that holds a bowl with lid. Heat for warming comes from a godet (ceramic vessel) which holds oil and a floating wick which is lit when heat is needed. *Photograph by Joanne Jennings, courtesy The Bidwell House Museum*

5. The Best Parlor—not yet decorated for the holidays—has a scrolled-arm wing chair, an upholstered Martha Washington style chair and a piecrust table. *Photograph by Paul Rocheleau, courtesy The Bidwell House Museum*

6. and 7. The Keeping Room door, and Keeping Room fireplace are decorated with wreaths during the holidays. *Photograph by Paul Rocheleau, courtesy The Bidwell House Museum*

8. A potash Kettle. *Photograph by Paw Rocheleau, courtesy The Bidwell House Museum*

# 24.

## Webb-Deane-Stevens Museum

Wethersfield, Connecticut

### A Connecticut Christmas

Christmas in Connecticut, this magical phrase conjures images—thanks to the movies, magazines and books—of handsome old houses knee-deep in freshly-fallen snow and agleam with candle-lit windows. Inside, beautifully decorated rooms are warmed by glowing fires and sparkling ornaments. Historic houses ensure that the image is no illusion, but a reality. The Webb-Deane-Stevens Museum invite all to share a real, authentic historic New England Christmas in Connecticut.

The Webb-Deane-Stevens Museum—located in the heart of Connecticut's largest historic district—consists of three authentically restored 18th-century homes that stand on original foundations, next door to one another. The 1752 Joseph Webb House served as George Washington's Revolutionary War headquarters in May 1781, when he met with French General le Comte de Rochambeau. The 1770 Silas Deane House was built for America's first diplomat to France. The 1788 Isaac Stevens House depicts life in the 18th and early 19th centuries through original family objects, and includes a new children's museum

Executive Director Charles T. Lyle says, "Visitors experience centuries of celebration when the Webb-Deane-Stevens Museum puts on its holiday finery and presents Christmas season tours of three homes that re-create the festivities of centuries past."

"On December 5, 2008," Lyle says, "doors opened for the museum's first annual preview party. The candlelight event included tours of all three elegantly decorated homes by costumed interpreters (guides, who provided insight on the lives and traditions of the families and how celebrations of the holiday season have evolved since the 1700s). Visitors were treated to musical entertainment, wine and hors d'oeuvres."

Decorations vary from year to year. "In 2007, the Joseph Webb House decorations reflected part of the Colonial Revival style of the 1920s and 1930s. In Year 2008, the Yorktown parlor included a tree with period ornaments, greens and flowers. The Northeast parlor was converted into a dining room bountiful with a holiday dessert course of sweets, cakes and puddings, along with pyramids of candy, fruit and nuts," says Lyle. "Other rooms featured period holiday decorations and ornaments from the 1920s. On the second floor, there was a large Christmas tree with an antique toy exhibit underneath."

Lyle notes that the Isaac Stevens Home in 2007 was decorated to depict holiday celebrations during the 1820s. "The front parlor featured a tabletop Christmas tree with candles and edible ornaments similar to what was done in the 1820s and 1830s. In 2008, the dining room was set for an 1820s holiday feast. On the second floor, the children's exhibits and toy museum featured 19th century clothing, toys and games."

Each year, there are surprises for holiday visitors to the Webb-Deane-Stevens Museum. "In 2007, for the first time in 70 years, visitors saw the Joseph Webb House drawing room's recently uncovered wall murals that had been installed in 1916 by Wallace Nutting, a previous owner of the Webb House. In addition to the Webb House, Nutting owned as part of his Chain of Colonial Picture Houses, four other important historic sites in New England that are portrayed in the wall murals.

"Also in 2007, on the second floor of the Isaac Stevens House, the new children's exhibits and toy museum (featuring 19th-century clothing, toys and games) opened for the holidays for the first time, adding excitement," says Lyle.

The 2008 surprise was the first time holiday opening of the *Silas Deane House* to visitors. The home's surroundings emphasized how the family celebrated the period surrounding New Years. "Then, those who were owed money invited their debtors into their homes and businesses to both settle their debts and partake of food, drink and conversation. A ledger of the period was on display as a memento of the financial activities of that period. Those activities have since evolved into our modern tradition of making personal New Years resolutions," says Lyle, "a fitting end to an authentic New England holiday."

One can only wonder what surprises future celebrations at the Webb-Deane-Stevens Museum hold for those who choose to celebrate Christmas in Connecticut.

**Opposite:** The failed Tea Room, opened by the Colonial Dames in 1922 as a museum fund-raising project. Furnishings and exhibit of needlework are based on photographs of that period. Holiday decorations are by the current staff. *Photographs by Charles T. Lyle, courtesy Webb-Deane-Stevens Museum*

Feast
for the eyes

# The Joseph Webb House

*T*he 1752 Joseph Webb house features a distinctive massive gambrel roof that permitted taller walls, more head room, and usable space so that the attic area. In this house, Mr. Webb and his second wife, Abigail, were such generous hosts, their house was known as Hospitality Hall. General George Washington and the French general Comte de Rochambeau met there to plan the subsequent Yorktown victory. Through the years, the house passed through various owners, including Walter Nutting who owned several historic houses that made up the *Walter Nutting Chain of Colonial Picture Houses.* Murals installed by Nutting in the hallway and front parlors remain to delight visitors.

The ca. 1752 Joseph Webb House, George Washington's headquarters in May 1781, was once owned by Wallace Nutting, an early preservationist. *Photographs by Charles T. Lyle, courtesy Webb-Deane-Stevens Museum*

1. The gracious stair in the First Floor Hall is decked in holiday garlands. *Photograph by Charles T. Lyle, courtesy Webb-Deane-Stevens Museum*
2. and 3. The Yorktown Parlor walls are decorated with a mural commemorating the surrender of the British army to George Washington at Yorktown, Virginia. Wallace Nutting commissioned the mural in 1916. Christmas decorations in 2008 reflected a 1940s Christmas, replete with tables set with refreshments. *Photographs by Charles T. Lyle, courtesy Webb-Deane-Stevens Museum*
4. and 5. The Northeast Parlor set set for a festive holiday desert affair. *Photographs by Charles T. Lyle, courtesy Webb-Deane-Stevens Museum*
6. George Washington slept here—quite literally—in the Northeast Bed Chamber of the Webb House during his five-day stay in May 1781. On the walls is the original 1750s wallpaper. *Photographs by Charles T. Lyle, courtesy Webb-Deane-Stevens Museum*
7. Antique toys are exhibited under the tree in the second floor hallway. The "Humpty Dumpty Circus" was manufactured by A. Schoehut and Company in the early 20th century. Collections of architectural banks, horsedrawn iron fire toys, and dog and cat doorsteps date from late 19th to early 20th centuries. *Photograph by Charles T. Lyle, courtesy Webb-Deane-Stevens Museum*
8. Treats and beverages were served in the Front Parlor of the Deane house to New Year's Day callers. The portrait is of Silas Deane's second wife, Elizabeth Saltonstall, by Joseph Blackburn, 1762. *Photograph by Charles T. Lyle, courtesy Webb-Dean-Stevens Museum*

# The Silas Deane House

$\mathscr{T}$he Silas Deane house, circa 1770, looks like the quintessential New England house. The spacious entry hallway opens into a best parlor, a back parlor, and a large kitchen. A gracious stairway leads to a second floor area that may have been used as a ballroom. The gracious house was built next door to the Webb house for Deane, a 1756 graduate of Yale College and a lawyer, who married Joseph Webb's widow in 1763. After her death, he wed socially prominent Elizabeth Saltonstall in 1769. Deane's involvement in Connecticut politics resulted in his being sent to France as America's Revolutionary War diplomat. While he was away, Mrs. Deane served tea to John Adams in 1774, and dinner to George Washington in 1776.

**Left:** The ca. 1770 Silas Dean House was built for America's Revolutionary War diplomat to France.
**Below, left:** Costumed singers perform in the Stairhall.
**Below, right:** A very simple evergreen and berry spray decorates the painted front door.

# The Isaac Stevens House

$\mathscr{A}$djacent to the Webb property is the house completed in 1789, for Isaac Stevens, a leatherworker. A center-hall Georgian floorplan, like the larger Webb house, the Stevens house boasts handsome woodwork and paneling—signs of affluence. Members of the Stevens family occupied the house for 170 years. Today, ground floor furnishings are typical of those of a middle class family circa 1820-1830. The second floor is furnished as it might have been when housing the Stevens five children.

The ca. 1789 Isaac Stevens House was built by a prosperous leatherworker. On the painted front door is a wreath embellished with colorful fruit.

1. In the Front Parlor is a traditional table top Christmas tree with period decorations, ca. 1840. Home-made ornaments include halved egg shells filled with cookies or candy. Candles on the tree burned only for about a half hour—wih fire buckets nearby—while the children received their presents. On the floor are examples of mass-produced toys available during this time.

2. The Bedroom on he second floor was occupied by five children. Five Christmas stockings hang at the foot of the beds—stuffed with an orange in the toe, edible treats, and small toys typical of the period.
3. The Connecticut Colonial Dames Collection of toys is exhibited on the second floor. *Photographs by Charles T. Lyle, courtesy Webb-Deane-Stevens Museum*
4. Springs of boxwood hang from the sash in a front window.

# 25.

## John Lind Home

New Ulm, Minnesota

### Christmas City Christmas

It's only fitting that the John Lind House, home of Minnesota's 14th Governor, be beautifully decorated for Christmas. After all, it is located in *Christmas City*—New Ulm, Minnesota, the town that kicks off the Holiday season each year with a Parade of Lights on the Friday following Thanksgiving.

For Christmas 2006, several merchants from around town contributed their time and talents to decorate this splendid house, creating a new sense of community spirit and expressing new appreciation for a house built by one of the town's most outstanding citizens.

The impressive Queen Anne house at the corner of Center and State Streets was built in 1887, by John and Alice Lind. Architect Frank Thayer designed the house which was built of local red brick above a rusticated stone base at a cost of $5,000. The characteristically asymmetrical massing featured a conical-roofed turret, bay windows with leaded stained glass transoms, and a wrap-around porch typical of the style.

The real story behind every historic house is the story of the people who built it. John Lind's story is that of a farm boy who became a teacher, lawyer, a three-term U.S. congressman, and the state's 14th Governor.

The Swedish-born Lind moved with his family to Goodhue County when he was 13 years old. A hunting accident cost young Lind his left hand. So instead of becoming a farmer, he began a career as a teacher, a school superintendent for several years, and went on to earn a law degree from the University of Minnesota and marry Alice A. Shepard. The Linds had four children, Norman, Jenny, Winifred, and John Shepard Lind. John's daughter, Alice Lind Griffith, has visited the Lind House many times and donated her grandfather's portrait, as well as a number of furniture pieces which were in the house when her grandparents lived there. Alice's grandson, William Griffith of Denver, was guest of honor at a 2005 Lind House Event billed as "Cocktails with the Governor." To the amusement of all, he came dressed as his great-grandfather, Governor John Lind! Another of John's daughter, Mary Lind Deppman, was a member of the U.S. Olympic Ski Team (about 1960).

As a young attorney, Lind was appointed to a position in the U.S. Land Office by President James A. Garfield. At age 32, Republican Lind won a seat in Congress—the first Swedish-born American to be elected to the United States House of Representatives. He served three terms before falling out with the party. As an advocate of unlimited silver coinage and the interests of the rural and urban working classes, and now a "political orphan," the two-time gubernatorial candidate was elected

**Opposite:** A large Christmas tree takes pride of place in front of the bow window in the ground floor Queen Anne turret area. The drop-leaf triangular table at left, used by the Linds, was donated to the house by a Lind granddaughter. *Decoration by Edelweiss Flower Haus, photograph by Mark Schneider & Mike Portner, courtesy of Lind House Association*

The John Lind House, built in 1887 for $5,000 in New Ulm, was the home of Minnesota's fourteenth governor.

Governor in 1899. John and Alice Lind remained in the Minneapolis/St. Paul area after his two-year stint as governor.

The Linds sold their New Ulm home in 1902, to a physician who made extensive changes to the interior. He upgraded the woodwork on the main floor to oak and built the Mission Style bookcases and benches. In 1927, he made drastic changes by converting the graceful dwelling into a duplex, with one apartment upstairs and one down.

In 1975, the John Lind Home as placed on the National Register of Historic Homes, cited for its architectural and political significance.

When the house came up for sale in 1983, the Lind House Association was formed for the purpose of purchasing and renovating the house, which had fallen into severe disrepair.

The Minnesota Historical Society advised the Lind House Association not to restore the house exactly to the Lind period, but rather to renovate the interior as a functional house. In doing so, the unfortunate changes made in the 1920s were put back to the way the house was originally. As a result of these efforts, "Many financial contributions and volunteer hours have gone toward restoring a former eyesore to its original splendor. The Lind House Association feels that if the Linds came back, they would find their house much as they left it," says Trudy Beranek, Manager of the historic site.

"Although the Lind House has been lovingly renovated in a style in which it was originally built, the house is not a museum. It serves as a home for the United Way offices, as a meeting place for local organizations, and is an ideal setting for private parties and receptions," says Ms. Beranek.

The Lind House is one of three former Minnesota governors' homes (along with the homes of Minnesota's first two governors, Henry Sibley and Alexander Ramsey, both located in St. Paul) that is open to the public. The Lind House is the only one owned by a private, non-profit organization—and to celebrate Christmas in Christmas City!

1. A Christmas tree with a child's sled at its base signals to citizens of New Ulm—known as Christmas City—that the John Lind House is decorated for the season's festivities by volunteers and local businesses who contribute time and resources. Photo by Mark Schneider & Mike Portner. *Photo courtesy of Lind House Association*

2. and 3. The second floor Queen Anne Turret Area features a tabletop Swedish Christmas tree with paper ornaments. The period child's rocker was a donation from its owner, the daughter of the second owner of the John Lind House. *Photograph by Mark Schneider & Mike Portner, courtesy Lind House Association*

4. The John Lind House—open to the public—is not a museum but more a community center! The Red Hat Ladies' annual lunch kicks off the Christmas season with a sing-along. Photo by Mark Schneider & Mike Portner. Photo courtesy of Lind House Association

5. Handsomely carved stairs leading from the Entry Hall to the second floor wear garlands of greenery and huge red bows. *Decoration by Edelweiss Flower Haus; photograph by Mark Schneider & Mike Portner. Photo courtesy of Lind House Association*

6. A plaque calls attention the landmark status of the house, listed on the National Register of Historic Homes.

7. In the Living Room, stained glass windows, the coal-burning fireplace (which has a new mantel), tiles, flooring, and wall sconce were original to the house. Other furnishings are antiques. A portrait of John Lind hangs above the mantel. *Decoration by Trudy Beranck and Kathy Filzen, photograph by Mark Schneider & Mike Portner, courtesy Lind House Association*

8. and 9. The children's play area is filled with toys, including a "play" ironing board and iron. *Photograph by Mark Schneider & Mike Portner, courtesy Lind House Association*

175

English country house tradition

# 26.

## *Maymont Mansion*

### Gilded Age Glory

To celebrate Christmas at Maymont is to return as a privileged guest to a splendid country estate of the Gilded Age—the age of Carnegie, Rockefeller, Vanderbilt and other fabulously wealthy barons of industry. Amazingly, this 100-acre estate on the banks of the James River remains exactly as it was during the lifetime of its founders, railroad magnate James Henry Dooley and his wife, Sallie May Dooley.

Centerpiece for Maymont ("May," Mrs. Dooley's maiden name and "Mont," French for hill) is the mansion built in 1893. Their Rome born-and-educated architect, Edgerton Stewart Rogers, combined heroic Romanesque Revival with romantic Queen Anne design elements to create the unique 12,000 square-foot, 33-room house. The monumental state-of-the-art structure boasted the most modern conveniences—electric lighting, an elevator, three full bathrooms, and central heat.

The Dooleys lived in this imposing home for 32 years. Maymont was bequeathed to the City of Richmond by the Dooleys (who had no children), following the death of Major Dooley in 1922, and Mrs. Dooley in 1925. In only six months after Mrs. Dooley's death, Maymont opened as a public park and museum. It has survived intact—an unusually complete example of a Gilded Age estate, including the residence, gardens, grounds and original architectural complex.

**Opposite:** A porte cochere provides cover from inclement weather for those arriving by carriage. *Photograph by Mike Weeks, courtesy Maymount Foundation*

An aerial view shows that Maymont Mansion in the heroic Romaneque Revival style with Queen Anne architectural elements, is centerpiece of a 100-acre estate with more than 25 original buildings preserved on the banks of Virginia's James River. *Photograph by Allen Jones, VCU Creative Services, courtesy the Maymount Foundation*

## About the House

*O*nce the mansion was completed, childless, 40-year-old Sallie Dooley devoted herself to creating a smoothly-functioning, sumptuously furnished home. Downstairs, in the English country house tradition, was the domain of a retinue of servants who kept the house working smoothly. Upstairs, the backdrop for James and Sallie, reflected the high style of the era, defined as "the juxtaposition and often asymmetrical arrangements of patterns, tones and textures, and historical and exotic styles."

Maymont literature tells a great deal about the interior design and outstanding collections.

Principal rooms each have distinct characters, clearly evident in twelve upstairs rooms seen on tour. The adjoining drawing rooms mirror French 18th-century styles. The walls of both rooms are covered in silk damask, the hearthstones are white onyx, and the friezes and ceilings are embellished with fine, ornamental plasterwork and decorative painting.

The small den is Near Eastern, and the living hall with its imposing English Renaissance-inspired mantelpiece brings to mind the "baronial hall" of romanticized history.

The library is a superb expression of eclecticism and "artistic" taste of the late 1880s and 90s. The ceiling and frieze are embellished with stencilling and strapwork carried out in mahogany, the wood used throughout the room, including the original Venetian blinds. The principal rooms are enriched by stained glass transoms, carved woodwork, and decorative ceiling and wall treatments.

The second floor includes a central living hall, lit by an immense Tiffany Studios stained glass window that rises above the grand stairway; the morning room, furnished with a painted satinwood set; the famous swan bedroom; two additional bedrooms; and two tiled bathrooms.

Maymount, 33-room mansion designed and built in 1893 by architect Edgerton Stewart Rogers, who was born and educated in Rome, was occupied by owners James and Sallie Dooley for 32 years. *Photograph by Tracey Crehan Gerlach, courtesy Maymont Foundation*

1.

2.

3.

# Christmas

*M*aymont is decked out in Victorian splendor for Christmas. Dale Wheary, Director of Historical Collections and Programs, says that no documents exist to reveal exactly how the Dooleys decorated. "The only Dooley Christmas decoration that has surfaced is a humble little Santa Claus and sleigh, donated by Mrs. Dooley's great niece. For Maymont Mansion, our decorating goal is to create a look that is appropriate for an upper class home of the 1890s, and visually impressive to suit the scale and opulence of the mansion...."

The Maymont calendar is filled with exciting events for the seven-week holiday season. In recent years, youngsters and adults from as many as 35 U.S. states and seven foreign countries have enjoyed the silent auction, holiday tours with costumed guides, wreath workshops, festive music, and marshmallow-toasting over a roaring fire.

Truly memorable is the moonlit horse-drawn carriage ride down the luminary-lit lane to the Maymont Mansion, which has become a favorite venue for romantic marriage proposals!

The French Normandy style Carriage House window boxes are decorated with greenery and red ribbon. *Photograph by Betty A. Sacra, courtesy Maymont Foundation*

1. The handsomely carved heavy entry door is decorated with garland, wreath, and tubs of seasonal greenery. *Photograph by Mike Weeks, courtesy Maymount Foundation*

2. Pink Drawing Room walls of silk damask are embellished with gilded swags. Architecture and furnishing are in the 18th century French style. The table is set for tea before the stunning fireplace with its gilded mantel and white onyx hearthstones. *Photograph by Dennis McWaters, courtesy Maymont Foundation*

3. In the Blue Drawing Room, walls covered in silk damask create a background of luxury for re-enacters wearing gowns popular during the Gilded Age. The Christmas tree, heavily decorated in glittering ornaments, drips with swags of beads. *Photograph by Dennis McWaters, courtesy Maymont Foundation*

4. and 5. In the Entry Hall, a beautifully carved wooden newel post supports a bronze lion. Above, a bronze caryatid holds a sconce. At right on the landing can be seen the 15-foot high Tiffany window that admits light to the 3-story staircase. *Photograph of entry by Dennis McWaters; photographs courtesy Maymont Foundation*

6. On December 7, 1912, the Dooleys hosted a luncheon at Maymont for Governors and their wives from all of the United States of America. At Christmas time, seasonal red ribbons would have hung from the chandeliers, reaching to the four corners of the Dining table. *Photograph by Katherine Wetzel, courtesy Maymont Foundation*

7. An elaborately decorated ornament is typical of vintage ornaments on Christmas trees throughout Maymont. *Photograph courtesy Maymont Foundation*

## Collections

*T*he provenance of the teapot, given to Benjamin Disraeli by Queen Victoria in 1878, may be questionable but other items are particularly noteworthy. These include a monumental Rococo Revival cabinet by Jean-Paul Mazaroz, shown at the Paris Universal Exposition of 1855, 18th C Gobelins' Don Quixote tapestry, and 17th C marble group by Francesco Grassia (a Bernini contemporary). Neuman and Company of New York's swan bedroom furniture is unique. One of the great treasures is the sterling silver and narwhal tusk dressing table and chair by Tiffany and Company of New York.

**Opposite:** Mahogany was the wood of choice for woodwork—including the fanciful strapwork ceiling and friezes—in the Library. Furnishings comprise a superb example of the period's eclectic taste. *Photograph courtesy Maymont Foundation.*
**Top:** The Dining Room's Exposition Cabinet, a monumental Rococo Revival piece by Jean-Paul Mazaroz of France, was shown at the Paris Universal Exposition in 1855. *Photograph by Katherine Wetzel, courtesy Maymont Foundation*
**Above:** The Carriage Collection, established in 1975, with the support of Elisabeth Scott Bocock, daughter of a business associate of Major Dooley, shows horse-drawn transportation typical of Virginia country estates 1893-1925. Recently, romantic Christmas carriage rides have prompted at least one marriage proposal. *Photograph by Mike Weeks, courtesy Maymount Foundation*

# 27.

## The Heard-Northington House
## Egypt Plantation

Egypt, Texas

### Lone Star Christmas

Not all plantation "big houses" look like Tara. Nor are they in the South. With no Gone-With-The-Wind-style Grecian columns, verandahs and balconies, the "big house" at Egypt Plantation, in Egypt, Texas, is historically significant. The State of Texas awarded the Heard-Northington House a State Historical Marker plaque and registered it with the Historical Landmarks for Texas. Lovers of Texas history—especially tidbits having to do with the historic Battle of San Jacinto—will find Egypt Plantation a fascinating place to visit during the Christmas holidays. Particularly since this house has its own Ghost of Christmas Past.

Welcoming visitors to Egypt Plantation today is owner and occupant of the 'big house," George Heard Northington IV. He is a direct descendant of Captain William Jones Eliot Heard, who fought at San Jacinto, and who in 1843 constructed what was then the "most historic big house in Wharton County."

Historian and author Janet Hobizal, Archivist of the Wharton County Historical Museum, says: "Captain Heard built the house at Egypt Plantation on the highest point of land. The style was called a double dog trot Georgian style, inspired by homes from his memories of childhood in Tennessee. There were no plans on paper; he and his wife, America, built it as they went along. 'Pillow talk' often determined the next days work.

"Walls—made of pink bricks crafted by plantation slaves using clay from the banks of nearby Caney Creek—were built twelve inches thick. They extend four feet into the ground, creating a solid foundation. For additional stability, metal tie rods extend through the attic to exterior walls, keeping all walls in secure alignment. Cypress doors and beams were brought from Galveston. Pine lumber, hauled from East Texas by ox-cart, was hand-adzed, to make 1-1/2-inch thick planks for flooring and ceilings. The comfortable house, completed in 1849, is kept cozy with two upstairs and two downstairs fireplaces.

"The German carpenters from Galveston who built the house also planted cedar trees in the front yard. Three of those magnificent trees remain today," says Janet.

There are many interesting artifacts in the "big house." Janet tells the story of one: As an officer, commanding Company F, Captain Heard fought at the historic Battle of San Jacinto. After Heard had left home to join the battle at San Jacinto, he sent back instructions to his family: "Put all the valuables in the family trunk. Take the trunk to the family cemetery and bury it. Mark the 'grave' with a sign saying, Died of Yellow Fever." Today, that trunk is in the front hall of the "big house" at Egypt Plantation.

Janet says that at the Battle of San Jacinto, Captain Heard was so close to the "twin sisters" (the Mexican Army's canons) that he was deaf in one ear for the rest of his life. "He and the men of his

**Left:** Captain Heard based the design of his 1840s dog-run colonial style house on buildings he had seen during his boyhood in Tennessee. *Photographs by Janet Hobizal, courtesy Egypt Plantation Museum*
**Opposite:** The Parlor

built it
as they along
went

company were the ones who fired the first shots at the enemy canons, killing all who were manning them. Because of Captain Heard and his men, the battle only lasted thirteen minutes." He returned home to Egypt and was probably present to dig up the trunk.

Like many intriguing houses, Egypt Plantation has its ghost. Captain Heard opened his home to wounded Confederate soldiers. Janet says, "One , while convalescing in an upstairs bedroom, vowed to always watch over Egypt. Sadly, he died in that bedroom. Today, his ghost is often heard in the house—Egypt's own Ghost of Christmas Past." Following Captain Heard's residency, six generations of the family have lived at Egypt Plantation (including the fourth George Heard Northington, the sixth-generation great-grandson who lives there today).

During that span of time, modern living quarters have been added to the rear of the house. But, the original structure reflects the era of plantations—a time when fertile soil made Egypt an agricultural center and Captain Heard built his 1836 cotton gin. (Just before the Civil War Captain Heard's son in law Mentor Northington built a new cotton gin, which the family operated for over 100 years.)

At that time, many prominent Texans lived in Egypt, including William Menefee (who signed the Texas Declaration of Independence), Dr. John Sutherland (Alamo courier), and Gail Borden (editor and inventor).

"That time and way of life now is visualized only in movies and books," says Janet, a Texas history expert whose GGGGrandfather was married to Thomas Jefferson's sister and is buried in the family cemetery at Monticello. Another of her great grandfathers was George Washington's uncle. Little wonder that Janet's impressive credentials include: Archivist, Wharton County Historical Museum; Member, Texas Historical Commission, Houston Archeology Association, and Houston Archivist Association; Historian, Glen Flora Spanish Camp Historical Society; Marker Chairman, Wharton County Historical Commission; Secretary/Treasurer, Historical Cemetery Preservation Association; Secretary, Egypt Plantation Museum. Who is more qualified to assure visitors that a Christmas visit to Egypt Plantation makes it possible to recapture a sense of historic time in a way that movies and books cannot.

## Slave Quarters At Christmas

*W*hen television producer Candi Flora was asked to produce a series of cable television shows commemorating *Black History Month, 2009,* she contacted Texas historian Janet Hobizal, Secretary of the Egypt Plantation Museum.

Janet says, "William Jones Eliot Heard, who started Egypt Plantation in 1832 with 2,222 acres of land, brought slaves along with his family from Georgia and Tennessee. Today, one slave cabin (circa 1840) and a bell used to call slaves from the fields remain at Egypt Plantation."

Ms. Flora arranged to film the one remaining slave cabin at the Plantation. To furnish the empty space as it would have looked at Christmastime in 1860, she brought along authentic items of that era. She narrated the film dressed as the occupant of those small quarters. "Earlier, for the Martin Luther King Day parade in Wharton, intrepid Candi had

Ms. Flora reenacts a scene showing a slave reading the Bible. Before Emancipation, Mrs. Heard taught slaves on the Plantation to read, despite Texas law which forbade it..

1. and 2. Six generations of Northingtons have gathered in the Parlor to play cards. The loveseat and several tables and chairs, including those in red velvet, are original to the home. In one corner is an antique organ.

3. and 4. The Dining Room was host to Sam Houston and Santa Anna—at different times, of course. Santa Anna occupied the house when the family was forced to abandon it during the "runaway" from his advancing army. Houston was a family friend. Original overhead oil lamps have been converted for electricity.

5. The original back doorway became a passageway to a new addition built in the 1970s for the Northington IIIs.

6. and 7. Entry doors, decorated with holly berry wreaths, are original to the house, so are the hardwood floors and ceilings, built from carefully-matched planks. The staircase—its original direction reversed so that children could not overhear conversations having to do with the Texas Revolution—is decorated in garlands made of evergreen ropes.

8. Near the front door is a Texas Historical Marker. Above the marker are lamps original to the building, decorated with greenery for the season. To the left of the doorway is the original brass bell used as a doorbell. Most window panes throughout are original wavy glass.

organized a live slave auction, replete with audience participation!" notes Janet.

Janet points out that like other Planters, Heard saw no contradiction between his Christianity and slave ownership. (After all, white Christians could argue that the Apostle Paul sent the Christian runaway slave Onesimus back to his master; forgetting—or not—Paul's admonishment in Colossians that masters give to their servants that which was *just and equal*.) "The Heards taught their slaves to read the Bible—even though that was against the law," Janet says.

The Heard-Northington family, which never bought or sold slaves in Texas, at one point sent their slaves via the 'underground railroad' to another state for protection. "They all returned to Egypt Plantation after the battle of San Jacinto," Janet says.

"I know that slaves who had become Christians would have decorated their quarters in some way to celebrate the birth of Christ. Pine branches and cones, plentiful in the area, would have been the meager but natural and beautiful decorations in these 1840s quarters," says Janet.

Television Producer Geneva Flora, dressed as a slave to reenact a documentary for Black History month, poses on the porch of the only remaining Slave Cabin in use at Egypt Plantation from 1840s to the end of the Civil War. Her program aired in February 2009.

wilderness

# 28.

## *Wade House*

Greenbush, Wisconsin

### A Simply Delightful Holiday

Simplicity—the polar opposite of the luxurious excesses of the elegant urban Victorian Christmas—can be found at Christmas at the Wade House in Greenbush, Wisconsin. This historic site has been preserved through the efforts of members of Wisconsin's internationally known and respected Kohler family and their Kohler Company.

At Wade House, according to House literature, it is possible to experience the beauty and simplicity of the mid-19th-century Christmas as celebrated by the earliest settlers of Greenbush. "Yankee and German traditions of the season, hands-on activities for young and old, stories, and horse-drawn wagon rides will forge memorable experiences while offering contrast to the celebration of Christmas today." A brief description of the history of this unique house by its director conjures images of the period when Wade House was created.

**Opposite:** Simple pleasures in the wilderness that was Greenbush, Wisconsin in 1844, included cutting down and bringing home the Christmas tree. *Photographs courtesy Wade House Historic Site*

Wade House, home to the Wade family and wayside inn to Wisconsin wilderness travelers, was rescued and preserved as a historic site by members of Wisconsin's civic-minded Kohler family.

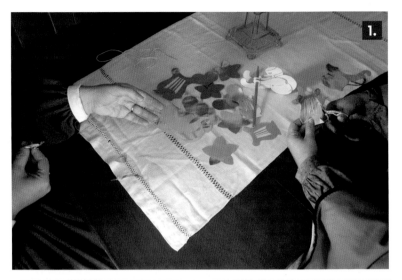

## *A Brief History*

$\mathscr{D}$irector David Simmons says, "When Sylvanus and Betsy Wade and their family came in 1844 to the area now known as Greenbush (between Fond du Lac and Sheboygan) it was a wilderness. This forward-looking couple came to establish both a home and a village beside a busy stagecoach trail. Four years later, Greenbush was a village with two stores, a sawmill, wagon shop, blacksmith, school and doctor. The Wades log home (in which they kept a tavern) was a regular stagecoach stop. In 1850, the Greek Revival style Wade House stagecoach inn opened."

David says that the inn was the scene of social, business, and political meetings and circuit court sessions. The taproom was a popular gathering spot. But, when the railroad came in the 1860s, it bypassed Greenbush. "Three generations of Wades lived at Wade House, which continued as an inn, until 1910. But in 1941, the house was sold to Mary Dorst, who wanted to restore the house to its 19th century state but by 1949 could not afford to continue restoration."

The narrative continues: "The Wade House in 1950 was basically unaltered but in bad shape when two members of Wisconsin's famed Kohler Company family—Marie Christine Kohler, daughter of the Kohler Company founder, and her daughter, Ruth De Young Kohler—entered the picture. Marie decided to restore the historic inn to its 1850s look, but died before she could get her plan underway. Her daughter, Ruth De Young Kohler, persevered and in 1950, the Kohler family and the Kohler Foundation bought Wade House and began its restoration," says David. Ruth De Young Kohler directed the restoration, accomplished deeding the property to the Wisconsin Historical Society, and opened the house to the public in 1953. Carl Sandburg attended.

Mary and Laurel surround parlor windows with garlands of fragrant greenery.

1. through 3. Handmade ornaments were both necessity and opportunity to express creativity. Tiny candles—usually burned only for a few minutes at a time—added mystery and excitement to the tree. Mary Martin, left, and Laurel Urven, right [blue dress with red lacing on sleeve], wearing period dress, add finishing touches to a tabletop tree.

4. The open-hearth Kitchen served up hearty, rib-sticking meals to family and guests.

5. and 6. Costumed musicians Matthew Harvey and Carol Jensen perform holiday music on vintage instruments.

# 29.

## Richards-DAR House

Mobile, Alabama

### An Antebellum Christmas

For Christmas with an authentic southern accent, one *must* visit the Richards-DAR House in Mobile, Alabama.

*Christmas at the Richards DAR House,* a fundraising event, kicks off the season the first week in December. The elegant house, lavishly embellished with porch-and-balcony posts and railings of lace-like wrought iron (in its famous four-seasons motifs), is always imaginatively and thematically decorated. For the *Riverboat Days when Cotton was King* theme, stalks of cotton, replete with fully-open fluffy white bowls adorned the elegantly curving stairway, Spanish Moss was draped across the windows, and art with river themes was displayed throughout.

Annually, holiday visitors are graciously greeted by hostesses in beautiful gowns befitting the antebellum period. Interiors transport visitors to days past but never forgotten in this house, which is listed on the National Register of Historic Places.

Board Member Sallie Grow describes Christmas at the Richards-DAR House. "Throughout the house during the holidays, the senses are delighted. There is the fragrance of fresh greenery, home baked goodies, and the sight of beautifully decorated trees with hand made ornaments. Several trees are decorated with themes that appeal to children and the child in everyone. Children are especially welcome during the holidays, and will appreciate the children's bedrooms chockfull of toys and teddy bears. These rooms are designed to inspire dreams of a visit from Santa (who may well be seated in the parlor)."

Ladies in Period costumes serve wassail and cookies to guests. "Music of the season performed by choral groups and local artists, adds to the Period ambience," says Sallie.

Everything about the Richards-DAR House—especially during the Christmas Holidays—recalls Mobile's golden age, the antebellum period. It was during that affluent period that a steamboat captain from Maine, Charles G. Richards, and his wife, Caroline Elizabeth (nee Steele) Richards (daughter of a wealthy planter), built their home. Captain and Mrs. Richards had twelve children, whose laughter some say they hear occasionally in the children's wing.

The 1860 Richards-DAR House, considered one of Mobile's finest examples of Italianate architecture, reflects the city's golden age. *Photographs courtesy Richards-DAR House Museum*

**Opposite:** The grandly-scaled Christmas tree fills one corner of the Living Room with its Cornelius chandelier.

Cotton was
KING

## About the House.

"*T*he Richards-DAR House, one of Mobile's finest examples of Italianate style architecture, is handsomely designed and decorated," says Sallie. "Architectural features recall the Greco-Roman influence. For example, the gracious reception hall and double parlors are fitted with massive chandeliers featuring fanciful mythological figures that hold sparkling etched glass globes. Front gallery flooring is classic gray and white marble. Mantels are carved from Carrara marble."

Notable are the ruby red panes of Bohemian glass that frame a doorway. Each room is fitted with silver servant-summoning bell pulls. One of the largest crystal chandeliers in Mobile hangs in the dining room. Furnishings throughout the house date prior to 1870, says Sallie.

In 1946, the Ideal Cement Company purchased the Richards House from descendants of Captain and Mrs. Richards, restored it, and used the house as downtown offices. In 1973, the property was presented to the city of Mobile, which leased the house to six Mobile Chapters of the Daughters of the American Revolution to furnish and administer as a historic house museum.

For its splendid accomplishments in maintaining the Richards-DAR House and preserving a precious part of Mobile's unique history, the six Mobile DAR chapters were awarded the Historic Preservation Project Award for the year 2004–2005 by the State Society.

One of the truly unique features of the Richards DAR House is the fine genealogical library compiled and maintained by the Governing Board of the House. It is open for research and copying of documents on the premises. "And, should a couple wishing to wed—adding to the city's genealogical history—the six Chapters of Mobile's DAR suggest a *Holiday Wedding* at the Richards-DAR House. "What could be more romantic?" Sallie asks.

The grand, sweeping staircase stars in the Entry Hall which is furnished with a box grand piano by Weber of New York City, c. 1860.

1.

2.

3.

4.

5.

6.

7.

8.

9.

1. In a formal sitting area, a large-scale French-style gilded mirror hangs above the rococo marble mantel.

2. Santa distributes gifts to re-enacters Mrs. Susan Tomlinson and her granddaughters Mia Milne and Corinne Gonzales. On the wall is one of a pair of mirrors shipped from France on a sailing vessel in 1852.

3. A circa 1840 mirror and a Baccarat crystal chandelier add sparkle to the Dining Room. The double-pedestal mahogany table is set for "Tea With The Captain."

4. Sallie Grow, spokesperson and hostess, serves tea to guests during a holiday event.

5. A bonnet (demi canopy) bed by Mallard is said to be a replica of Napoleon's bed.

6. The wreath-decorated door of the house built by Captain Charles Richards.

7. and 8. In a spacious, light-filled bedroom, guide Sheila Shell folds a vintage quilt.

9. In the Master Bedroom with its beautifully carved four-poster bed, guide Sheila Shell smooths a pillow, in preparation for visitors.

*Photographs courtesy Richards-DAR House*

exuberant

# 30.

## Campbell House

### Meet Santa in Saint Louis

*M*ark your social calendar—the Campbell House at 1508 Locust Street in Saint Louis, Missouri, extends an invitation to come calling at Christmas!

Celebrate the holiday season in a house visited by President Ulysses S. Grant, General William Tecumseh Sherman, and Red Cloud. Yes, Red Cloud! The great Sioux Chief was a "tribal brother" of Robert Campbell, the Irish immigrant *cum* wealthy fur trader who bought this house in 1854.

What great fun to walk through stately doors into the elegant entry with its grand nine-foot tall hall mirror and marble sculpture—just as President Grant, General Sherman, and Chief Red Cloud did. Stroll through gracious rooms filled with fine furnishings. And while guest won't be sitting on the same chair as President Grant or Red Cloud, it is probably there. About ninety percent of the furnishings in Campbell House today were purchased by Robert and his wife Virginia during their residency (1854 to 1938).

Executive Director Andrew Hahn says, "After the recent completion in 2005 of a five-year, $3 million restoration, the Campbell House Museum now stands as one of the most accurately restored mid-19th Century buildings in America. It reflects the high-Victorian opulence of the 1880s."

Victorian décor was designed to thrill. Leading specialists directed the restoration of interiors whose exciting colors have been described as bright, fresh, and used in combinations that seem contemporary. Flamboyantly patterned textiles, wallpapers, and carpets are a world away from latter day patternless, monotone-colored textiles relieved only by subtle texture.

The "too much is never enough" exuberance of the mature Victorian style of Campbell House interiors influences the Christmas decor. Together, furnishings and decorations set the stage for celebrating high holidays in high style.

**Above:** The façade of the Campbell House Museum, restored to its 1885 appearance—when it was at the heart of St. Louis' first private street, Lucas Place. *Photographs courtesy Campbell House Museum*

**Opposite:** The portrait bust, a plaster copy of the marble original by Antonio Canova, is of Pauline Bonaparte Borghese.

1. The long narrow Entry Hall of the Campbell House features an ancient Roman marble bust and distinctive set of gothic revival chairs. The distinctive neo-Greco painted wall decoration was the result of a restoration project completed in 2005; the 9-ft. tall pier mirror with half-inch mercury glass was restored and reinstalled by Jente Woodworking in 2008. Nearby is a commissioned copy of an original painting by George Caleb Bingham, whose home is also featured in Christmas at Historic Houses. *Photographs courtesy Campbell House Museum*
2. and 3. The Morning Room with its four leaded-glass windows was added to the house in about 1880. Attached to the dining room, it served as an informal parlor. A side table holds an English Rockingham tea service.
4. The master Bedroom is handsomely furnished with carved furniture of the period, and has an ornately patterned carpet.

## Christmases Past

*T*he Campbells hosted holiday dinners for family, friends, and employees and their guests. A 1890 photograph of the Campbell dining table shows a centerpiece of sculptures of Santa and all his reindeer, including "Vixen." A "Vixen" sculpture was given to each guest as a table favor.

"In 1985, a 'Vixen' was donated back to Campbell House by the family who had received it at the 1890 dinner. They had used it on their Christmas table for more than 90 years," says Mr. Hahn.

Rita Heller Willey, whose aunt was a friend of Mary Boerste, the housekeeper, recalls attending a party given by a son, Hugh Campbell on Christmas Day 1922. "I was 13 at the time, the youngest guest... There were paper hats for

# Brief History

$\mathcal{T}$he Campbell house is not merely a 19th Century version of a designer showcase. It is an important repository of the inspiring history of a man who built companies, communities, and a country. Some 500,000 pages of family records and an album of 60 photographs of the house by son Hugh, an amateur photographer, document the history of family, house, and city.

Campbell came to the United States as an 18-year old Irish immigrant and started work as a fur trader in the Rocky Mountains. His adventures—akin to those of his friends Kit Carson and Jedediah Smith—prompted Washington Irving to write, "His exploits partake of the wildest spirit of romance. No danger or difficulty can appall him."

He expanded his interest in furs to a network of business, including dry goods, banks, hotels, real estate and steamboats. Campbell gave Samuel Clemens (Mark Twain) his first river boat to pilot, which Clemens promptly sank.

In addition to helping make St. Louis the nation's fourth largest city during his lifetime, Campbell was instrumental in creating Kansas City. But he made St. Louis his home and built his mansion in Lucas Place, then a new suburb developed for homes of the wealthy. Campbell House, the only 19th Century survivor, is now surrounded by 20th Century commercial buildings.

Mrs. Campbell, eighteen years younger than her husband, reportedly spent $40,000 for parlour furniture on one Philadelphia shopping trip alone. But, Robert was a very wealthy man, worth $500 million in current dollars at his death in 1879. (Mrs. Campbell died in 1882.) Furnishings continued in use until the death in 1938 of Hazlett, a reclusive schizophrenic and the last of three children (James, Hugh and Hazlett) who had survived to adulthood. (Ten other Campbell children had each died before their eighth year.)

In honor of James, the house was bequeathed to Yale University. As part of its celebration of its 50th anniversary, in 1942, Stix, Baer and Fuller—a local department store and St. Louis institution—purchased the house from Yale and presented it "to the people of St. Louis through the Campbell House Foundation."

In 2008, the National Society of the Daughters of the American Revolution (NSDAR) dedicated a plaque marking the Campbell House as a NSDAR recognized historic site.

**Right Column:** The Parlor is the most formal and fashionable room in the Campbell house. The six suites of Rococo revival furniture were purchase by Virginia Campbell in Philadelphia in the summer of 1855. A magnificent pair of gasoliers with their original shades, is by the renowned firm of Cornelius and Baker. The room's ornately painted wall and ceiling decoration is the result of the 2005 restoration.

everyone. Mr. Campbell played the square piano made of rosewood. Later there were musicians and dancing. I ... have the table favor I received ...a pin-cushion in the form of a nickel-plated shoe with green velvet insert."

Ms. Willey says, "On one occasion when my brother Ferd and I were small children, we visited Mary at 1508 Locust, and Mr. Hugh told us to pick a toy from the Christmas tree. I still have the celluloid doll I picked and the celluloid horn my brother selected." Today, toys are an important part of the museum's Christmas exhibits.

The Victorian inspired Christmas tree in the Parlor Room, decorated with Italian angels, has an elaborate crèche scene at its base.

1. through 3. In 1873 and 1874, President and Mrs. Ulysses S. Grant were entertained by the Campbells in this Dining Room, at this table which seats eighteen. The massive marble-top sideboard is decorated with fish, birds, fruits and a stag head. "Vixen," the large decorative reindeer was one of many given as a party favor to each family attending a circa 1890 dinner party. This one was donated back to Campbell House in 1985 by members of the family who had received it at the 1890 party and used it to decorate their Christmas table for more than 90 years.

# Holiday Events

$\mathscr{A}$ nticipate an event-filled Christmas season at the Campbell House. For a complete calendar of events, check with Campbell House and/or the web site. Traditionally, there are *two musts:*

The holiday theatrical performance by the resident theatre group, Etc. Senior Theatre Company (and party) is extraordinary. In 2008, the troupe performed *A Child Christmas in Wales* by Dylan Thomas. The year before, they did Dicken's *A Christmas Carol.*

Of course, the Holiday Candlelight Tour in conjunction with some of the other historic houses in St. Louis is a thrilling occasion.

In the Exhibition Rooms, special Christmas exhibits of antique Christmas decorations and toys include a traditional early Victorian tabletop tree surrounded by cast iron toy horse and buggies, rare French toys (including the doll in a goat cart and a milkmaid), and bride and groom porcelain-head dolls.

welcome all

# 31.

## *Hearthside Homestead*

Lincoln, Rhode Island

### Christmas By The Hearth

Where could one sit beside a cozy fire on Christmas Day and be warmed by flames and flute-like music, *both* emanating from the *fireplace*? Perhaps only one place in the world—Hearthside Homestead in Lincoln, Rhode Island.

"The draft of the fire causes the wind-driven *Pandean Pipes*, an extraordinary musical instrument built into the fireplace chimney, to produce clear musical notes," says Kathy Hartley, founder and president of Friends of Hearthside. "Such instruments have been found in *castle* ruins in Europe, but it would be rare, perhaps impossible, to find them installed in a *house* anywhere other than at Hearthside Homestead."

Why were the *Pandean Pipes* installed in the Hearthside parlor chimney? "Installing this unique musical instrument may have been just one more attempt by Stephen Smith, who built this house for his lady love, to give her the most wonderful house in the nation. To woo her with music, and live happily ever after with her at Hearthside," she says.

Alas, *happily ever after* was not to be. Kathy tells the story:

In 1810, Stephen Hopkins Smith of Smithfield, Rhode Island (which became Lincoln in 1871) set his heart on marrying the daughter of a prominent Providence family.

**Above:** Stephen Smith built his 1810 house of locally-quarried fieldstone. The distinctive ogee curve of the gable roof is repeated in the dormer and the roof of the side portico.

**Opposite:** An elliptical over-door fan light and sidelights admit light into the Entry Hall. A costumed guide opens the heavy paneled door to holiday callers. On the wall of the well-furnished hall is a collection of prints by David Davidson, noted for his hand-colored photography, including photographs he took of Hearthside around 1920.

# Dinner Menu for

Large Turkey with Homemade Stuffing
Gravy
Creamed Potatoes-and-Onions
Yellow Squash
White Turnips
Tiny Peas
Old-Fashioned Bread and Butter Pickles
Large Pitted Black Olives
Small Green Olives
Cranberry Sauce

Candlight, lace, and a wreath dress up a Dining Room window with its handsome wooden shutters folded into the deep reveal of the 14-inch thick exterior cut-stone wall.

She told him she had her heart set on 'marrying well' and 'expected to live in the grandest house around.'

When Smith (affluent but not wealthy) won $40,000 in a lottery, he kept his windfall a secret and prompted by love, began building a grand house. As the story goes, one Sunday afternoon Smith took his buggy to Providence and invited the young woman to take a drive with him. They set out at a leisurely pace, eventually turning onto Great Road. As the crossed the bridge over the Moshassuck River, Hearthside

came into view. 'Oh what a beautiful house!' she exclaimed. Smith's hopes soared. Then she added, 'But, I could never live so far out in the wilderness!'

Smith turned the buggy around, returned to Providence, and never courted her again. He settled in a house down the street, and built a business (the Butterfly Mill, now the Butterfly House) across from Hearthside. This sad story of love and rejection was cited in *Ripley's Believe It or Not*, which referred to Hearthside as *The Heartbreak House.*

Since is completion in 1814, twelve families have lived in Hearthside. Most recently it had been the home of Andrew and Penelope Mowbray and their three children, young Andrew (Drew), Sherry and Stuart. Theirs is a much happier version of Smith's story. One day, Andrew drove Penelope past Hearthside. 'Oh,' she said, 'What a beautiful house! And look it's even for sale!' Hearthside was home to the Mowbrays for 40 years.

The senior Andrew died in 1996, and Mrs. Mowbray sold the property to the Town of Lincoln. Now, under the stewardship of Friends of Hearthside, Hearthside is truly *The House That Love Built.*

The Mowbray's love for the Christmas season continues at Hearthside today in special holiday events, beginning with the early *December Candlelight Christmas Tour.* Candles in the window guide guests to a hospitable house beautifully decorated by volunteers to evoke memories of Christmases past. "In keeping with the candle-in-the-window to welcome travelers tradition," says Kathy, "there is no admission fee. Instead, guests donate non-perishable food to the Rhode Island Community Food Bank." Guides dressed in Victorian finery greet guests who stroll through elegant rooms, while a harpist plays seasonal music.

Drew Mowbray, eldest of the three Mowbray children and now residing in Germany, recalls to Kathy fond Christmas memories of his childhood years (1950s-1970s) at Hearthside.

The tree used to be put up in the parlor (the room with the Pipes of Pan). One year, the Christmas tree was to the right of the fireplace, but most often it was placed in the corner next to the door going out to the front hall. We children were shooed upstairs on Christmas Eve, but if

# Mowbray *Every-Christmas*

Apple Cider
Eggnog
Tea in the Pot

Homemade Pumpkin Pie
Homemade Apple Pie & Extra Sharp Cheese

Wainscoting and the mantel in the Dining Room are made from old window shutters that were installed during the 1920s. The metallic gold of chargers and the russet colored cloth at table, and topiaries on the sideboard add holiday glamour.

someone forgot to close the door to the parlor below, and we lay down on the floor and peered through the banister, we could sort of see a bit of the tree.

We put out cookies and milk in the front hall or the kitchen for Santa. For a number of years, my father took the time and made his own Christmas cards, painted on canvas, and then printed up the cards at his business, Mowbray Printing Company. One of my favorites was the one with Santa flying over the houses on Great Road, and Hearthside was shown in a "cut-away" view so you could see all the family inside—adults trimming the tree and we kids sleeping upstairs.

My father fed an interest in collecting by giving me so many neat buttons or buckles from the Civil War that he had found during the year. I looked forward to these antiques and still have all of them. One year, I received a young boy's Civil War uniform jacket, which I also still have.

Friends' Christmas cards were hung on a cord across the fireplace mantle, and there were always electric candles put in the windows to make the house look so nice. It seemed that the snow was always very deep. We could slide from the little hill in the field behind the house all the way to the back steps. In the 1960s, all our friends would turn up at the house, so it was full of long-haired teens. Good memories to say the least. We always had turkey. And eggnog—with something forbidden in it. The house was alive.

Sherry Mowbray remembers her father painting the scenes for the Christmas cards when she was a young girl in the early 1960s," says Kathy. "She also fondly recalls how lovely the white candle-style lights in each window looked from the outside—especially when there was snow on the ground; how it helped set the mood inside. Sherry liked to go around to each room and turn the candle bulbs on.

"Sherry told me, 'Our tradition was to cut our own Christmas tree—always getting one just a bit too big, even though the ceilings at Hearthside were quite high.' Her favorite part of Christmas dinner was her mother's apple pie," says Kathy.

## The House

*H*earthside—built of fieldstone and trimmed with granite quarried from a ledge across the street from the house—is considered one of the finest examples of Federal architecture in Rhode Island. It is listed on the National Register of Historic Places. A replica of Hearthside was displayed in the Rhode Island Pavilion at the 1904 World's Fair in St. Louis.

In 1905, the Talbot family named the house *Hearthside* because of its ten fireplaces. They named their hand-weaving business conducted there "Hearthside Looms," and Hearthside became known throughout the country for the quality of the goods woven there. Hearthside has captured the hearts of those who maintain it as an important historic house museum and a vital link to Lincoln's past, present and future. It welcomes all—especially at Christmastime.

The Gazebo, an anniversary gift from Andrew Mowbray to his wife, Penelope, becomes winter garden sculpture when silhouetted against new-fallen snow. *All photographs by Ruth A.B. Clegg, Angell Fine Arts; courtesy Hearthside Homestead*

1.

2.

3.

4.

1. The ca. 1890s hand-carved mahogany four-poster tester bed is the focal point of the Master Bedroom. Poinsettias, Christmas trees, and lights in the stained-glass log holder add cheer to the cozy room.
2. An antique mahogany sleigh bed sets atop impressive wide plank floorboards in a Front Bedroom.
3. Reproductions and antique greeting cards are hung as ornaments on Christmas trees in the Master Bedroom.
4. Christmas trees at Hearthside are decorated with exquisite glass ornaments.
5. The fireplace in the Front Parlor (the family den) contains the "Pipes of Pan," pipes activated by the draft from the fire to create flute-like notes or music.

5.

# Hearthside's Mowbray Christmas Cards

*Kathy Chase Hartley, neighbor and childhood friend of the Mowbray children, recalls receiving original Mowbray Christmas cards. Now these charming cards are reproduced for sale in the Hearthside Homestead Gift Shop.*

*I* can still remember the excitement and anticipation I had as a little girl in the 1960s experiencing all the traditions of the Christmas season in my own home. To me, what was almost as exciting as counting down the days until Christmas by opening the little door on the Advent Calendar each day, was the trip down our long driveway to the mailbox with my mother. We would return home, sit down and open each envelope and look at the holiday cards...pictures of Christmas trees, wreaths, Santa Claus, and latest photos of families and relatives...pretty typical holiday cards. But it was the Christmas card from the Mowbray family that I would most eagerly await each year.

The Mowbray family card was so special. It was as though the card was made just for us! After all, it was a card with scenes from my own street, Great Road! Each year, the card was so different, receiving it was just like the surprise of opening a present. While all the other cards were set aside in a neat pile, the Mowbray card was given a special spot for display in our house, becoming part of the decorations of the season. Some 50 years later, we still have the cards!

The cards were the creation of Andrew Mowbray, who designed and painted each one as an oil painting on canvas and then had prints of them made into cards. He kept his paintings a secret. Not even his family knew what the subject of the painting would be each year until it was completed and he unveiled it to them.

My all time favorite card was the *View of Hearthside*. The cut-away view was like peering into a dollhouse—except this one was a real house, just around the corner from my house! And there was Santa Claus flying right overhead, probably right before he would visit me. I could see my friends in the card, Drew and Sherry Mowbray tucked away in their beds upstairs. Their father was downstairs decorating the Christmas tree in the parlor, and their mother in the kitchen taking something out of the oven... maybe it was apple pie! There was even a cat in the house. I studied that card for hours it seemed. Hearthside always held a special mystique for me. This card was mesmerizing with this cozy scene. You could get lost in it, imagining yourself being a part of that wonderful home on Christmas Eve.

I remember the S*katers on Butterfly Pond*, the pond across the street from my house! There were men, women and children dressed in old-fashioned clothes skating on the pond and looking so very elegant. I skated on that pond too, but their clothes were far different from my corduroy pants and ski parka. The women wore long skirts, hooded capes and fur muffs, and the men wore fancy jackets and top hats. Even the kids looked dressed up in their Sunday best to skate in! Looking closely at the card, it was no wonder...the date is 1814. It is probably the way Christmas might have looked when the first family lived at Hearthside.

I also liked the *Great Road Christmas 1812* card, because it also had so many other houses and buildings along Great Road besides Hearthside. It was fun to look at it and guess whose house was where on the road, and whose house had not yet been built. It was yet another card to let your imagination take you along the journey up Great Road during the olden days, and bring you to stop at Hearthside to get warm by the fires inside. I never noticed until now that there was a mistake on the card. It was in the Great Road sign where the "r" was mistakenly left out of "Christmas." The discovery of it was devastating to Andrew. From that point on, he quit the family tradition of having custom painted Christmas cards, so the *Great Road Christmas* card was the end of an era. For me, waiting for Christmas to come never seemed quite the same again.

*Wishing you an Old Fashioned Merry Christmas and a New Year of Happiness*

*Penny, Andy, Drew and Sherry Mowbray*

Reproductions of these original Christmas cards by Andrew Mowbray are now available in the Hearthside Manor Gift Shop.

# 32.

## Riversdale House

### Calling on the Calverts

George and Rosalie Calvert's elegant Federal-era Riversdale House (1801) in Riverdale Park, Maryland (a Washington, D.C. suburb) is the scene of this much-anticipated annual event. It continues a centuries-old, popular Federal-era tradition—the winter season social call.

"Mid-winter was the height of a season dedicated to socializing, including calling (short visits), dinners, balls and so on. These events occurred not on one day only, but throughout the winter," says Ann Wass, Ph.D., Historian, The Maryland-National Capital Park and Planning Commission (M-NCPPC).

"For the festive *Calverts by Candlelight* event, the Riversdale Historical Society and the Paint Branch Garden Club decorate the house with greenery (mainly *faux* for practical reasons). The

M-NCPPC Greenhouse and Nursery Unit supplies poinsettias and paperwhites (white narcissus), since Mrs. Calvert cultivated bulbs. Costumed interpreters reenact scenes typical of the Calvert's residency as visitors tour the candlelit house at their own pace," Ann states. "A harpist plays holiday airs and popular songs of the period and Riversdale's knowledgeable docents are on hand to answer questions."

"Our education coordinator and food historian, Joyce White, sets the dining room table for the supper that would follow a ball—dining and dancing were two favorite forms of entertainment during that period," she points out.

George and Rosalie Calvert were socially prominent. George was a grandson of the fifth Lord Baltimore, of

Luminaries guide visitors to Riversdale under the stars. The stucco-covered Federal era manor house, built in 1801 by Henri Joseph Stier, was given to his daughter, Rosalie Stier Calvert in 1893.

winter season
*social call*

Riversdale staff member Maria Grenchik, dressed in her Federal-era gown, pauses on the Grand Staircase as she prepares to welcome holiday guests. *Photographs by Cassi Hayden, courtesy Riversdale House Museum*

1 and 2. In the Dining Room, frankly *faux* fruit centerpieces similar in style to those seen in the Governor's Mansion in Williamsburg, decorate the dining table which is set for dinner. Generally, during the holiday season, Riversdale is decorated simply with fresh greenery, as it would have been when occupied by the Calverts—a period when Christmas was not universally celebrated in America. *Photographs by Cassi Hayden, courtesy Riversdale House Museum* 3. *Faux* (fake) foodstuffs typical of the era are used as seasonal décor at Riversdale, since real food is costly, will not last the duration of the holiday period, and attracts unwelcome pests. Fake food for use in historic houses was developed to perfection by Winterthur, as reported in *Discover Yuletide at Winterthur*, 1998, Henry Francis du Pont Winterthur Museum, Inc.

Maryland's founding family. George's sister, Eleanor married George Washington's stepson, John Parke Custis. Rosalie was the younger daughter of Henri Joseph Stier, a wealthy immigrant from Antwerp.

"In her January 11, 1819, letter to her sister, Isabelle van Havre, Rosalie wrote about Washington's *sparkling winter social scene*. 'We have been to three very splendid private balls, one at Mr. Tayloe's, the others at Mr. Bagot's [the British minister] and Mr. de Neuville's [the French minister].' She mentioned two dinners planned for Riversdale, and a 'fine luncheon' at which there would be dancing," Ann notes. "Rosalie also stated that at elegant dinners guests sat down to dine at 5:00 o'clock, but there's no mention of the time guests left the table!"

At Riversdale today, in addition to setting a formal table in the dining room, Joyce re-creates an open hearth kitchen and guests may grind spices and mix dough as she cooks over the open hearth. Joyce makes Martha Washington's *Great Cake* to serve to guests.

Joyce adds, "Fragrant odors of cinnamon in mulled cider and nutmeg in homemade cookies, along with the warmth of the hearth fire, stimulate the senses, helping to re-create the mood of that time period. Young visitors can add to the ambience by creating their own early American souvenir—a clove-studded pomander."

New Year's events figured significantly in the Calvert's holiday season.

"When the Calverts launched their oldest daughter, Caroline, into society, her first appearance was at the White House—Open House on New Year's Day, 1818," says Ann. "Rosalie's letter to Isabelle, dated January 8, 1818, mentions that Mrs. Monroe received the Calverts very graciously. That and Rosalie's other letters, held in the Riversdale Historical Society archives, were translated from the original French, edited by Margaret Law Callcott and published as *Mistress of Riversdale*, Johns Hopkins University Press, 1991

For the New Years, "the Calverts and Stiers exchanged gifts—tulip bulbs, tulip-poplar seeds, books, prints of views of Niagara Falls, and ribbons, and other baubles," Ann says, "but probably not on Christmas Day."

Ann notes that Christmas was not universally celebrated in the United States during the time that the Calvert family lived at Riversdale (1803-1838). "Interestingly, Mary Boardman Crowninshield (whose husband, Benjamin, was Secretary of the Navy) brought her two oldest girls to Washington to be with him the winter of 1815-1816. In a letter to her mother in Salem, Massachusetts, she wrote: 'Christmas morning [1815]. It seems more like our Independence—guns firing all night. I am going to the Catholic Church—it is their great day.' Although Riversdale does not celebrate Christmas Day, Mrs. Calvert was from Flanders, so we celebrate Sint Niklass (the Flemish equivalent of Santa Claus) Day."

4. Walls of the Library/Study with built-in bookcases are covered in French wallpaper. Over the mantel is a bust of George Washington.
5. Fruit and greenery brighten the overdoor, as it would have in the early 1800s.
6. Windows and the canopy bed are hung with toile, a French fabric that adds pattern and color to the somewhat austere and decidedly elegant bedroom.

# Brief History

*D*r. Wass recounts briefly the history of Riversdale:

**1801** – Construction of Riversdale, now a National Historic Landmark, was begun by Henri Stier, a wealthy Flemish aristocrat who, with his family, had fled the French Revolutionary armies.

**1803** – Napoleon Bonaparte declared amnesty for *émigrés* and Henri and his family returned to Antwerp. Henri gave the uncompleted house to his younger daughter Rosalie, who in 1799 had married George Calvert, a tobacco planter and descendant of Maryland founder Lord Baltimore.

**1821** – Rosalie died at Riversdale at age 43 (having borne nine children, five of whom lived to maturity).

**1838** – George Calvert (who never remarried) died. The Calverts' second son, Charles Benedict Calvert, continued living at Riversdale. A scientific farmer, he founded the Maryland Agricultural College (now the University of Maryland, College Park) and, as a U.S. congressman, sponsored legislation establishing the U.S. Department of Agriculture.

**1864** – Charles Calvert died and eventually his widow Charlotte went to live in Baltimore. Riversdale began to decline.

**1887** – The estate was sold to developers laying out a commuter suburb of Washington, DC, that they named Riverdale Park. The mansion was at first company headquarters, then a boardinghouse, then a country club, and finally William Pickford owned and modernized the house before leasing it to U.S. Senator Hiram Johnson, former Governor of California.

**1920s-30s** – U.S. Senator Thaddeus Caraway of Arkansas bought the house, died in office, and his widow, Hattie, completed his term, ran for the seat, and became the first woman elected to the Senate. She could not afford to continue living there and the house was sold to Abraham Walter Lafferty, a former congressman from Oregon.

**1949** – Lafferty sold the property to the Maryland-National Capital Park and Planning Commission, which used Riversdale as offices. The Riversdale Historical Society advocated for preservation of the house and the Calvert family cemetery, occasionally showing the house to the public.

**1988** – A full restoration of the house began. Rosalie Calvert's letters were found in the family archives in Belgium, sparking the decision to restore the house to its appearance during Rosalie and George Calvert's occupancy (1801-1838).

**1993** – Riversdale was opened to the public!

Today, during the Christmas Holidays, the Calverts' Riversdale is ready to receive callers who will experience a pre-Victorian Christmas in a decidedly historic house.

David Mallinak, a living history interpreter, portrayed the Calvert children's tutor during one holiday event at Riversdale.

celebrating
creole Style

# *33.*

## *Gallier House*

### Christmas in the French Quarter

Hurricane Katrina caused great havoc in New Orleans, but the French Quarter and its Gallier House (associated with the Hermann-Grima House) miraculously suffered only minor damage. Both Houses re-opened to the public on December 12, 2006.

At these venerable homes, December is the busiest time of an event-filled year. Christmas is the climax of the year's exciting educational and events calendar designed to promote the city's history and culture during the period 1830 to 1880.

A visit to the Gallier House (and its counterpart, the Hermann-Grima House)—French Quarter landmarks—is to catch a glimpse of Christmas as it was celebrated in 19th Century New Orleans. Call this Christmas Creole Style—unique in the United States.

The Louisiana French of 19th century New Orleans observed Christmas as a religious holiday. French families attended midnight mass at St. Louis Cathedral and went home to a reveillon breakfast. This "simple" meal included

The 1857 Gallier House on Royal Street in New Orleans boasts the lace-like filigree ironwork synonymous with the city's French Quarter. *All photographs courtesy Hermann-Grima/Gallier Historic Houses*

various egg dishes, jellied meat or "daube glace" and rich cake with cream.

Among the Creoles, Christmas morning began with a visit from Papa Noel, often a relative, who would distribute small gifts and trinkets to the children. Creches (nativity scenes) were an important part of the French Catholic Christmas. On Christmas Day, children and adults would visit several churches to observe the elaborate nativity scenes.

Gentlemen set aside New Year's Day for their annual formal visits to friends and relatives. Ladies usually stayed at home to receive calls, which started as early as 11:00 a.m. Displayed prominently in the parlor were cake and eggnog. In anticipation of the endless rounds of callers, dining room tables were filled with an assortment of pastries and confections. The centerpiece (an ornamental cake or sugar sculpture) was often ordered from a confectioner's shop. These works of art were shaped into exotic forms such as a Chinese pagoda or a Gothic church. The table was also filled with other desserts, such as sweetmeat pyramids, cookie cones, birds nests made of orange peel, and brightly colored marzipan.

On New Year's Day, elaborate gifts were exchanged. New Orleans shops and warehouses were filled with children's toys for the holidays. Adults received gifts as well. Jewelry, books and decorative pieces like fans were popular.

After New Year's, Epiphany, a religious feast day, was observed by Catholics on January 6th (twelve days after Christmas) to commemorate the manifestation of Christ to the Magi. The tradition of hiding a token in a cake was a symbolic reenactment of Epiphany. The brioche, a sweet pastry, concealed a bean and later the figure of a baby. This custom was combined with the secular tradition of giving a Ball at which a king and/or queen was chosen on Twelfth Night.

**Opposite:** A portrait of the architect James Gallier hangs above the marble fireplace which is decorated with gilded pinecones and evergreen garlands.

The 1857, Victorian-style Gallier house, at 1132 Royal Street, home of noted New Orleans architect James Gallier, Jr., represents the 1860-1880, post-Civil War era lifestyles of its affluent, successful designer. The Woman's Exchange purchased this house in 1996. It is now considered an outstanding example of historic restoration. The earlier 1831 Federal style Hermann-Grima residence at 820 St. Louis Street was purchased in 1924. It first served as a place where women of any income bracket could sell their handicrafts on commission. The house served as chaperoned housing for single women. In the 1960s, the Woman's Exchange decided to restore the house, which has the *only outdoor kitchen and horse stable in the French Quarter.* Today, this house depicts the 1830-1860 lifestyle of a prosperous Creole family. Alas, there are only snapshots of this splendid house, but add it to a tour of the Gallier House!

Especially at Christmas time, both the Gallier and the Hermann-Grima houses welcome all to a unique Creole Christmas in New Orleans.

1. and 2. The lace-covered table in the Dining Room is laden with fancifully-decorated holiday treats.
3. Simple greenery adds a subtle holiday note to the elegant Back Parlor with its ornately embellished frieze and imposing gilded pier mirror.
4. A tea table in the Front Parlor is set for holiday entertaining.
5. In a child's bedroom, colorful candies and a tiny table set for tea are hints that Christmas has arrived at the historic Gallier House.

In the simply designed Kitchen, baskets with plaid-ribbon bows are filled with holiday foods in preparation for gifting.

# 34.

## Monticello

Charlottesville, Virginia

### A Day of Greatest Mirth and Jollity

Monticello, an architectural gem, may be America's most-studied structure. Thomas Jefferson's lifelong passion and masterpiece defines neo-Classicism in all the timeless elegance that invites revisiting—time and again in all seasons, none more wonderful than Christmas.

Reference to past Christmases at Monticello are rare. According to Mindy Keyes Black, Monticello Department of Development and Public Affairs, in *"Christmas at Monticello,"* November 1996, in his 1762, diary, Thomas Jefferson described Christmas at Monticello as "The day of greatest mirth and jollity." A holiday moment was recorded by Jefferson himself on Christmas Day in 1809. As he watched the spirited play of his eight-year-old grandson Francis Wayles Eppes, he wrote: "He is at this moment running about with his cousins bawling out 'a merry Christmas,' 'a Christmas gift'…."

Christmas celebrations today respect the authentic—with no hint of Victorian excess—still, for Christmas 2006, something new was added to Christmas at Monticello—*Holiday*

*Signature Tours*—which offered visitors a rare treat indeed, an opportunity to experience Monticello after dark.

A variation of popular Signature Tours, the hour-long guided tours of this much-celebrated house offered visitors an intimate leisurely look at how the house typically would have been

**Above:** A Christmas Season snowscape underscores Jefferson's neo-Classic design of Monticello, his country home near Charlottesville, Virginia that has become a design mecca. *Photograph by Robert C. Lautman, courtesy Thomas Jefferson Foundation*

**Top:** Luminaires light the path to festivities at Monticello as they were during the Christmas holiday season when Jefferson was at home there. *Photograph by Robert C. Lautman, courtesy Thomas Jefferson Foundation*

Exotic
fresh fruits

decorated and holidays celebrated at Monticello. While curators do not know *exactly* how the house was decorated, they do know from other sources that 1700s holiday decorations and celebrations would have been considerably "more modest than today's."

Socializing—important to Virginia culture and a major impetus for holiday decorations—was the highlight of the winter season in what was essentially an agrarian society freed by cold and snow from the demands of planting and harvesting. At one time, Jefferson's daughter wrote of their hosting a prodigious number of guests: "Our lives are literally spent in the drawing room."

For the Christmas 2006 Holiday Signature Tours, rooms on the main floor, including the parlor, were adorned with "authentic period decorations." Virginians in Jefferson's day decorated their homes in the English manner. This meant that bits of greenery—in the forms of wreaths, garlands, and swags—would have enlivened interiors. Perhaps berries and fruits would have added color to greenery at Monticello as they did in Williamsburg. (Historians note that lavish holiday celebrations and unbridled decorating were not the order of the day in America's early years. Christmas trees and other holiday traditions such as hanging stockings derived from a variety of customs that emerged during the 19th century, and became commonplace much later, during the Victorian era.)

Essentially, Christmas during this period throughout Virginia was a time for "fellowship and feasting."

Monticello's *Holiday Evening Tour* included displays of *faux* food that showed what the Jefferson family would have served to guests during the season. Special foods served in beautifully appointed rooms were a highlight of convivial gatherings during this season. Beautiful porcelain dinnerware and handsome silver tableware from the Monticello collection adorned tables.

A table of tempting desserts was exhibited in the Tea Room, all well-documented Monticello recipes. The dessert course of any holiday meal in the late 18th or early 19th century was a feast for the eyes and taste buds. Displays were arranged for color, proportion, and height, as well as for tempting the sweet tooth. Among the holiday treats of that period was a dessert called Snow Eggs. This dish of meringue in a bed of custard was a favorite dessert in early 19th-century Virginia. At Monticello, it was made by James Hemings, an enslaved cook who trained in Paris during Jefferson's years there as a statesman.

Another traditional holiday dessert was mince pie—a mélange of apples, raisins, spices, and beef suet—popular during this particular season. Perhaps Jefferson had mince pie in mind when he placed the following order for apples. "I will take the liberty of sending for some barrels of apples, and if a basket of them can now be sent by the bearer they will be acceptable as accommodated to the season of mince pies," he wrote to Mary Walker Lewis on Christmas Day, 1813.

Displays in Monticello's kitchen also showed other favorite dishes served during Jefferson's life. Included was the classic French custard, Crème Brulée. Honoré Julien, Jefferson's chef at the President's House, is believed to have developed the recipe.

Christmases and all Jefferson's days at Monticello inspired these lines: "I am as happy no where else and in no other society, and all my wishes end, as I hope my days will end, at Monticello."

Simple decorations of evergreens decorate the mantel in the Parlor, chandelier in the Entrance Hall, and areas throughout the house. *Photographs by Robert C. Lautman, courtesy Thomas Jefferson Foundation*
**Bottom, Left:** In the Tea Room, fresh fruits—exotic in Jefferson's day—are the only hint of a holiday season that was celebrated with inward enthusiasm and little outward display. *Photographs by Robert C. Lautman, courtesy Thomas Jefferson Foundation*

*Photographs by Robert C. Lautman,
courtesy Thomas Jefferson Foundation*

*M*any wonderful decorative products inspired by (and sometimes exclusive to) particular historic houses are available in an on-site gift shop, on-line, and via catalogs. Visiting the shops—a marvelous way to end a historic house tour—makes it possible to bring a bit of Christmas home.

The Travis House Candle Lantern holds a 1-1/2-in. pillar candle or tea light. The lantern and a matching wrought-iron hook are hand-made. For information: Williamsburg Products, 1-800-446-9240,. www.williamsburgmarketplace.com. *Photograph courtesy The Colonial Williamsburg Foundation*

1.

2.

10.

3.

4.

9.

1 and 2. Lang Building Ornaments in fine porcelain capture the distinct charm of historic Williamsburg's buildings. Included are Pasteur & Galt Apothecary, Bruton Parish Church, King's Arms Tavern, Wythe House, Barber Shop, Ewing House, Nicolson Store, Courthouse and Christiana Campbell's Tavern. Ornaments may be purchased separately or as a set. For information: Williamsburg Products, 1-800-446-9240,. www.williamsburgmarketplace.com. *Photograph courtesy The Colonial Williamsburg Foundation*

3. The image of the John Lind House on the collectible ornament is by the Chinese artist Long Zhang. For information contact: lindhouse@newulmtel.net.

4. Berry Candle Rings add instant charm to classic Sarah Coke Candlesticks (found at the Coke-Garrett House site) which come in assorted heights. For information: Williamsburg Products, 1-800-446-9240,. www. williamsburgmarketplace.com. *Photograph courtesy The Colonial Williamsburg Foundation*

5. A vintage Christmas Card painted by Andrew Mowbray, former resident of Hearthside Homestead has been reproduced for sale in the Gift Shop. *Photograph by Ruth A.B. Clegg, Angell Fine Arts, courtesy Hearthside Homestead*

6., 7. and 8. Inside the Hearthside Homestead Gift Shop there is a world of wonderful gifts and decorative accessories. *Photograph by Ruth A.B. Clegg, Angell Fine Arts, courtesy Hearthside Homestead*

9.. and 10. Items that say Mount Vernon range from ornaments to china to paintings and much more! Contact: ww.mountvernon.org.

5.

8.

7.

6.

# Gift Shops and Historic Houses

Adams House
22 Van Buren Street
Deadwood, South Dakota 57732
Tel: 605.578.3724
adamsmusuemandhouse.org

Baldwin-Reynolds House
(PO Box 411)
639 Terrace Street
Meadville, PA 16335
Tel: 814.671.1030
jsherretts@baldwinreynolds.org

Bartow-Pell Mansion Museum
895 Shore Road, Pelham Bay Park
The Bronx, New York 10464
Tel: 718.885.1461
info@bpmm.org

Bidwell House Museum
100 Art School Road
PO Box 537
Monterey, MA 01245
Tel: 413.528.6888
bidwellhouse@gmail.com

Billings Farm and Museum
5302 River Road, P.O. Box 489
Woodstock, Vermont 0509
Tel: 802.457.2335
www.billingsfarm.org

Biltmore Estate
1 Approach Road
Asheville, North Carolina 28803
Tel: 800.624.1575 or 828-225-1333
www.biltmore.com

Bingham-Waggoner Home and Estate
313 West Pacific
Independence, Missouri 64050
Tel: 816.461.3491
Fax: 816.461.1540
www.bwestate.org

Blithewold Mansion,
Gardens and Arboretum
101 Ferry Road
Bristol, Rhode Island 02809
Tel: 401.253.2707
www.blithewold.org

Butterworth Center
1105-8th Street
Moline, Illinois 61265
Tel: 309.765.7970
www.butterworthcenter.com

Calvin B. Taylor House Museum
PO Box 351
208 North Main St.
Berlin, MD 21811
TaylorHouseMuseum@Verizon.net

Campbell House Museum
1508 Locust St.
St. Louis, MO 63103
Tel: 314.421.0325
campbellhm@earthlink.net

Campbell House
2316 W. First Avenue
Spokane, WA 99204
Tel: 509.456.3931
themac@northwestmuseum.org

Charleston Museum
(Joseph Manigault House)
360 Meeting St.
Charleston, SC 29403
Tel: 843.722.2996, x 235
www.charlestonmuseum.org

Chief Vann House Historic Site
82 Georgia Highway 225 N
Chatsworth, Georgia 30705
Tel: 706.695.2598
www.gastateparks.org/info/chiefvann/

Chinqua Penn Plantation
2138 Wentworth
Reidsville, NC 27320
Tel: 336.349.4576
lisa@chinquapenn.com

Colonial Williamsburg Foundation
P. O. Box 1776
Williamsburg, VA 23187-1776
Tel: 757.229.1000
www.history.org/history

Crocker House Museum
15 Union Street
Mount Clemens, MI 48043
Tel: 586.465.2488,
Fax: 586.465.2932
crockerhousemuseum@sbcglobal.net

David Davis Mansion
1000 E. Monroe Drive
Bloomington, Illinois 61701
Tel: 309.828,1084
Fax: 309.828.3493
davismansion@yahoo.com

Deere-Wiman House
817-11th Avenue
Moline, Illinois 61265
Tel: 309.765.7970
butterworthcenter.com

Drayton Hall
3380 Ashley River Road
Charleston, South Carolina 29414
Phone: 843.769.2600
draytonhall.org

Egypt Plantation Museum
(Heard-Northington House)
PO Box 219
Egypt, TX 77436-0219
egypt@wcnet.net
www.egypttexas.org

Emlen Physick Estate
1048 Washington Street
Cape May, NJ 08204
Tel: 800-275-4278 or
609-884-5404
Fax: 609-884-2006
Email: mac4arts@capemaymac.org
www.capemaymac.org

Florence Griswold Museum
96 Lyme Street
Old Lyme, CT 06371
Tel: 860-434-5542
www.flogris.org

Gallier House
(Hermann-Grima & Gallier Houses)
20 Saint Louis Street
New Orleans, LA 70112
el: 504.525.5661
Email: HGrimaGallier@aol.com
hgghh.org

Hazelwood Historic House Museum
1008 South Monroe Avenue
Greenbay, WI 54305
Tel: 920-437-1840
bchs@netnet.net
www.browncohistoricalsoc.org/
hazelwood

**Below, Left:** The Gift Shop at the David Davis Mansion offers goodies galore for the holiday shopper. Contact: davismansion@yahoo.com.
**Below, Right:** The Leu House and Gardens Gift Shop in Orlando, offers Christmas season and year-'round gifts and decorative accessories. Information: www.leugardens.org.

Hearthside Homestead
677 Great Road
Lincoln, RI 02865
Tel: 401.726.0597
kathy.hartley@hearthsidehouse.org

Hearthstone Historic House Museum
625 W. Prospect
Appleton, WI 54911
Tel: 920-730-8204
www.focol.org/hearthstone

Hermann-Grima & Gallier Houses
20 Saint Louis Street
New Orleans, LA 70112
Tel: 504-525-5661
HGrimaGallier@aol.com
www.hgghh.org

Joel Lane Museum House
PO Box 10884
Raleigh, NC 27605 (US mail)
728 W. Hargett St.
Raleigh, NC 27603
Tel 919-833-3431
Fax: 919-833-9431
joellane@bellsouth.net

John Lind Home
622 Center Street
New Ulm, MN 56073
Tel: 507-354-8802
lindhouse@newulmtel.net
www.thelindhouse.com

Joseph Manigault House
350 Meeting Street
Charleston, SC
Phone: 843-722-2996
info@charlestonmuseum.org
charlestonmuseum.org

Lyndon Baines Johnson Ranch
P.O. Box 329
Johnson City, TX 78636
Tel: 830-868-7128
www.nps.gov/lyjo/

Leu House Museum
1920 N. Forest Avenue
Orlando, FL 32803-1537
Tel: 407-246-2620
Fax 407-246-2849
rbowden@cityoforlando.net
www.leugardens.org

Marshal's Home and Museum
217 North Main Street
Independence, MO 64050
Tel: 816.252.1892
www.jchs.org.

Marjorie Kinnan Rawlings Farm
18700 South CR 325
Cross Creek, FL 32640
Tel: 352-466-3672
marjoriekinnanrawlings.org

Maymont Mansion
1700 Hampton St.
Richmond, VA 23220
Tel: 804-358-7166, x 329
info@maymont.org
www.maymont.org

Molly Brown House Museum
1340 Pennsylvania Street
Denver, CO 80203
Tel: 303-832-4092
Tel: 303-832-2340
www.mollybrown.org

Monticello
P.O. Box 316
Charlottesville, VA 22902
Tel: 434-984-9822
www.monticello.org

Morris Butler House
1204 North Park Avenue
Indianapolis, IN 46202
Tel: 317-636-5409
Fax: 317-636-2630
Email: mbhouse@historiclandmarks.org
www.historiclandmarks.org

Mount Clare
Carroll Park
1500 Washington Blvd
Baltimore, MD 21230
Tel: 410-837-3262
www.mountclare.org

Mount Vernon
Mount Vernon Ladies' Association
PO Box 110
Mount Vernon, VA 22121
Tel: 703-780-2000
www.mountvernon.org

My Old Kentucky Home
(Federal Hill)
501 East Stephen Foster Avenue
Bardstown, KY 40004-0323
Tel: 502-348-3502
MyOldKentuckyHome@ky.gov
parks.ky.gov/findparks/

Oldfields–Lilly House and Gardens
4000 Michigan Road
Indianapolis, IN 46208-3326
Tel: 317-923-1331
www.ima-art.org

Petersen House Museum
1414 W. Southern Avenue
Tempe, AZ 85282
tempe.gov/petersenhouse/

Pettengill-Morron House
1212 W. Moss Avenue
Peoria, IL 61606
Tel: 309-674-1921
Fax 309-674-1882
www.peoriahistoricalsociety.org

Physick House
(Emlen Physick Estate)
1048 Washington Street
Cape May, NJ 08204
Tel:: 800-275-4278 or
609-884-5404
Fax: 609-884-2006
mac4arts@capemaymac.org
www.capemaymac.org

Pittock Mansion
3229 NW Pittock Drive
Portland, OR 97210
Tel: 503-823-3624
www.pittockmansion.com

Richards-DAR House Museum
256 North Joachim Street
Mobile, AL 36603
Tel: 251-208-7320
2638smbg@bellsouth.net
www.richardsdarhouse.com

Riversdale House Museum
4811 Riversdale Road
Riverdale Park, MD 20737
Tel: 301-864-0420
Ann.wass@pgparks.com
www.pgparks.com

Roseland Cottage (Bowen House)
556 Rte. 169,
Woodstock, CT
www.historicnewengland.org

Samuel Cupples House
at St. Louis University
3673 West Pine Mall
St. Louis, MO 63108
Tel 314-977-3575
Fax 314-977-3581
cupples.slu.edu/x436.xml

The Sherwood-Davidson House
Museum
Veterans' Park
PO Box 785
Newark, OH 43058-0785
Tel: 740-345-4898
sherwooddavidson@yahoo.co
www.lchsohio.org

Slifer House Museum
80 Magnolia Drive
Lewisburg, PA 17837
Tel: 570-524-2245
Gary.parks@albrightcare.org
www.albrightcare.org/slifer-house

Tudor Place
Historic House & Garden
1644 31st Street NW
Washington, DC 20007
Tel: 202-965-0400
Fax: 202-965-0164
info@tudorplace.org
www.tudorplace.org

Vaile Mansion - De Witt Museum
1500 North Liberty
Independence, MO 64050
Tel: 816-325-7430
www.vailemansion.org

Van Cortlandt Manor
525 South Riverside Avenue
Croton-on-Hudson, NY 10520
Tel: 914-271-8981
Email: info@hudsonvalley.org
www.hudsonvalley.org

Waddesdon Manor
Nr Aylesbury
Buckinghamshire
HP18 OJH
United Kingdom
Tel: +44(0) 1296 658586
Fax: +44(0) 1296 653212
waddesdonmanor@nationaltrust.org.uk
www.waddesdon.org.uk

Wade House
W7824 Center Street
PO Box 34
Greenbush, WI 33026
Tel 920-526-3271
Fax? 920-526-3626
David.simmons@wisconsinhistory.org
www.wadehouse.org

Webb-Deane-Stevens Museum
211 Main St.
Wethersfield, CT 06109
Tel: 860-529-0612, x14
clyle@webb-deane-stevens.org
www.webb-deane-stevens.org

White House
1600 Pennsylvania Avenue
Washington, D.C. 20500
Tel: 202-456-7041
White House Visitor Center,
Southeast corner of 15th & E Streets
www.whitehouse.gov

Whitehall
Henry Morrison Flagler Museum
One Whitehall Way
P.O. Box 969
Palm Beach, FL 33480
Tel: 561-655-2833
www.flaglermuseum.us